ADVANCE

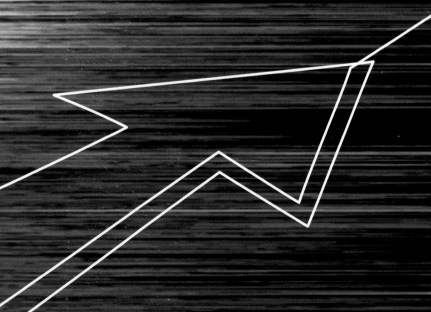

ADVANCE

THE ULTIMATE
HOW-TO GUIDE
FOR YOUR CAREER

BY
GARY BURNISON
CEO, KORN FERRY

WILEY

Library of Congress Cataloging-in-Publication Data:

ISBN 9781119641773 (Paperback) / ISBN 9781119641780 (ePDF) / ISBN 9781119641766 (ePub)

PRINTED IN THE UNITED STATES OF AMERICA

V10014293_092719

BOOK DESIGN & PHOTO ILLUSTRATIONS
ROLAND K MADRID & CANDACE DODDS

FRONT COVER DESIGN & ILLUSTRATION
JONATHAN PINK

[Alice] was a little startled by seeing
the Cheshire Cat sitting on a
bough of a tree a few yards off. . . .

"Would you tell me, please, which
way I ought to go from here?"

"That depends a good deal on
where you want to get to,"
said the Cat.

"I don't much care where—"
said Alice.

"Then it doesn't matter
which way you go,"
said the Cat.

Alice's Adventures in Wonderland,
Lewis Carroll

**TO ALL WHO FEEL STUCK
IN THEIR CAREERS AND DON'T
KNOW WHERE TO GO.**

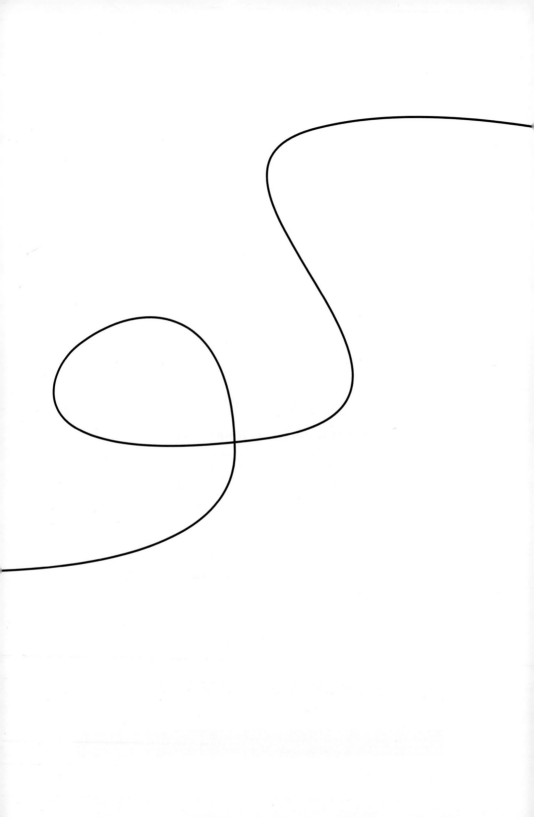

Contents

I HATE MY BOSS.

MY COWORKERS ARE
FROM MARS.

NO PROMOTION
AND NO RAISE IN SIGHT.

IT'S DEATH BY
MEETING IN THIS PLACE.

CAREER DEVELOPMENT
IS A JOKE.

I CAN'T WAIT FOR
JURY DUTY—OR PERHAPS
JAIL TIME WOULD
BE BETTER.

MAYBE I'LL BE LUCKY
ENOUGH TO GET THE FLU!

I BEG YOU...

CAN YOU GET ME OUTTA HERE ?

NOT SO FAST... IT COULD BE YOU!

You may think that getting ahead is 90 percent what others can do for *you*. Wrong! That 90 percent is what you do for yourself and for *others*.

Too many people today are helplessly passive when it comes to their careers. Maybe they think the company will develop them or they'll be plucked out of the sea for some fabulous new opportunity.

The truth is, you get hired for what you can do but fired for who you are. So if you want to get ahead, start there—figure out who you are and the value you bring.

Job tenure today is a whole new ball game. These are the days of the *career nomad*, traveling from one opportunity to the next, whether inside or outside the company.

The numbers tell the story. On average, people spend about four and a half years in each job. Think about it—that's barely the time you spent in college, and less than the life span of most TV sets. Tenure for younger professionals, who for a variety of reasons aren't interested in hanging their hat at one place for too long, is even shorter: as little as one or two years. To put this in context, I will have about four jobs in my career. My five millennial children will each have about 30.

It's no surprise, then, that the term "job-hopper" is no longer a pejorative. Being a "free agent" is the new reality. Two years in a job equates to two old-school annual performance reviews. That's hardly enough time to be passive. To thrive, you need to take control!

Long gone are the days when success meant dutifully sticking to one company and moving up the ladder slowly, with a retirement party and a gold watch at the end. That's what companies used to encourage. In those days, companies rewarded folks who were loyal, dishing out better pay, bigger bonuses, and corner offices with each promotion.

Today, there is no office. And the career development ladder has been mostly yanked away.

Careers are more like labyrinths. Sometimes moving ahead involves looping around first with lateral assignments to add breadth and depth. Don't fight it—embrace it, because this dynamic is here to stay. This shift dramatically changes the parameters of how to manage careers.

But the fact is, people spend more time doing research when buying a flat-screen TV or a washing machine than thinking about how to get ahead in their careers.

It's time to take control! No one is coming to your rescue.

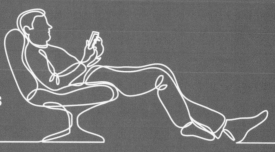

Anything *Except* Advancing Their Careers

OVER THE COURSE OF A LIFETIME, THE AVERAGE PERSON SPENDS:

10,625 days looking at a digital device

7,709 days sitting down

1,769 days socializing

240 days laughing

180 days exercising

90 days on the toilet

1 day crying

9,490 days sleeping

730 days commuting…

But not nearly enough time thinking about a career.

From where I sit, as the CEO of a global consulting firm that develops 1.2 million people every year and puts someone in a job every three minutes, I believe everyone can take control of their career—if they're willing to do the hard work.

I wrote this book because the world of work is going through these dramatic changes, but the traditional career advice to guide people hasn't kept up. There are millions of people like you who feel stuck and don't know what to do. Or else they move from job to job, without a real plan of where they're going.

In the following pages, I draw on my own experience as well as

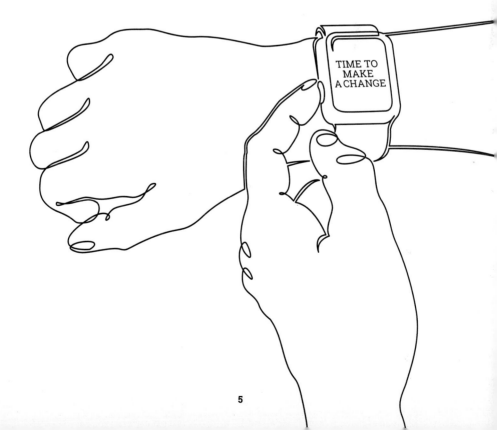

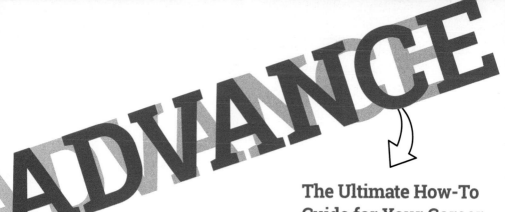

The Ultimate How-To Guide for Your Career gives you a wealth of practical and actionable advice. You'll have what you need to take control of your career, starting today.

the perspectives and intellectual property of Korn Ferry, which has more than 50 years of expertise in recruiting and developing talent. Those five decades have allowed our researchers and scientists to compile more than six million data points on what behaviors get people ahead and which don't. And we have a very unique resource, Korn Ferry Advance (*KFAdvance.com*), which acts like a gym membership for your career, providing constant care and nurturing to advance professionally.

Simply put, why not take advice from the ultimate insiders? If you do, it will make a real difference in how you think, act, and interact, so you can take control of what will become an amazing career.

Surely you can invest time in your career. You have the time, so why not use it wisely? William Penn said it best: Time is what we want most, but what we use worst.

So if you're ready, let's begin.

Advance is organized into three sections:

IT STARTS WITH YOU...

1 Awareness awakens! Before you do anything else, you need to look in the mirror. What are your values, motivations, strengths, and blind spots? Know yourself and manage yourself first so you can make a bigger and better impact. You must have a plan.

...BUT IT'S NOT ABOUT YOU

2 Unless you're a sculptor working alone in your studio, chipping marble or molding clay, you aren't a solo performer. Despite all the technological advancements of the past few decades, we still need to work with others. Doing that requires emotional intelligence and interpersonal skills—especially when dealing with that boss you hate and those annoying coworkers.

TO EARN MORE
YOU NEED TO LEARN MORE

3 It isn't like microwaving popcorn on high. Advancing your career takes time and effort. That only happens by being a lifelong learner, driven by insatiable curiosity. You need to be learning agile—the number one predictor of success.

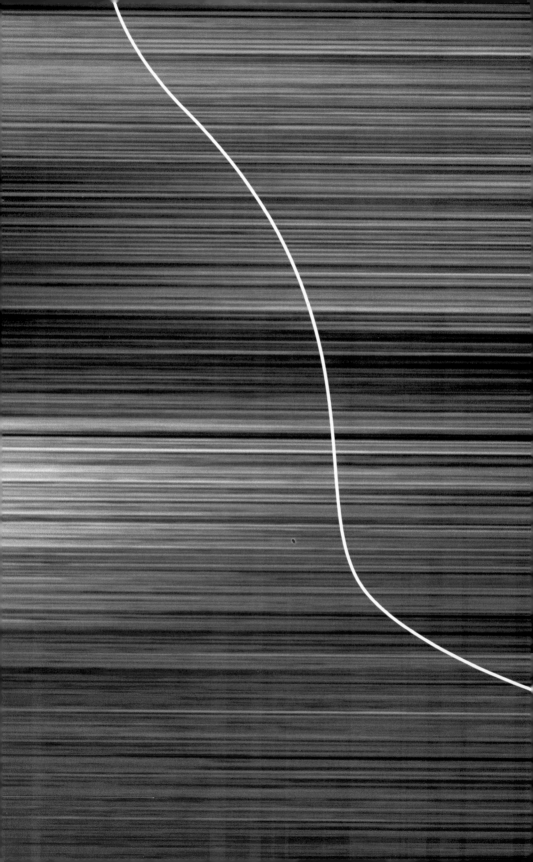

Part One

IT STARTS WITH YOU...

You get hired for what
you can do but fired for
who you are. So if you want
to get ahead, start there—
figure out who you are and
the value you bring.
Awareness awakens!

Chapter One

TAKING CONTROL:

It's Harder Than You Think

I'll never forget the date: September 4, 1984. There I was in my Brooks Brothers suit and my shiny new wing tips, carrying the hard-sided leather briefcase that was empty except for a handful of pens and pencils. Having grown up in a small town in Kansas, I'd never been in a skyscraper office building before I went on job interviews. But as a graduate of the University of Southern California and having passed the CPA exam,

I was fortunate enough to receive several job offers from accounting and consulting firms. When I walked through the heavy oak door of Peat Marwick Mitchell (today's KPMG), I felt like I'd arrived—until I met all the others.

There were 125 of us in that year's class of new hires, and that was just in the Los Angeles office. Then they gave us the speech: Within two years, 50 percent of us would be gone—and even more within four years. Only one or maybe two of us would ever make partner.

Things started to change with the first assignment: Global merger? Massive restructuring? Takeover attempt? Nope—moving boxes.

EARLY ON, I NOTICED HOW CERTAIN PEOPLE AT THE CONSULTING FIRM STOOD OUT BECAUSE THEY JUST "DID IT." THEY HAD "HUSTLE."

I heard others complain, but I had worked summers in college as a mover—although not in a suit that I couldn't afford to get dirty. I moved boxes all week, from office to office and between floors. When I was done with the boxes, I was given a phone book and a 10-key calculator and told to add the rows of phone numbers to sharpen my 10-key skills. Ridiculous busywork? For sure. But I did it without complaint because that's what I was asked to do.

Early on, I noticed how certain people at the consulting firm stood out because they just "did it." They had "hustle." Over the years, I've noticed how hustle and hunger quash pedigree every time—even if someone is an Ivy League graduate or has a PhD. It's been shown that people who have to scramble in their careers not only do well (and often better than their pedigreed peers), but they learn from their failures and end up in a career that yields greater satisfaction. If things are too easy or if privilege opens all the doors, the result can be misery and discontent—no matter how much money you earn.

All my young life, I hustled: delivering newspapers, painting houses, working construction—you name it. It wasn't that we were poor; it's just that we didn't have any money. There is something about seeing, as a kid, all the furniture being repossessed and taken from the house that chills your bones. That image reminds me daily of where I came from and, more importantly, who I am.

My first *real* assignment at KPMG was doing inventory in a cavern-ous warehouse. My trial by fire was accepting (and drinking) a cup of coffee from the warehouse manager in a dirty mug he pulled straight out of the sink. As if to sanitize it a little, he ran the mug under the faucet for two seconds and used his fingers to wipe off the dirt. In doing this, I earned the respect of that warehouse manager, who saw that I wasn't just another college grad who wouldn't get his hands dirty. I had done this type of work before, from crawling over pallets to scaling piles of boxes.

Flash-forward nine years after that first job: I was among fewer than a handful of people from my Los Angeles "class" at the firm who made partner. Flash-forward 23 years to 2007: I became CEO of Korn Ferry. So much has changed in that time—successes and failures, all lessons I've embraced.

At the top of the lesson list: take control. You can't expect others to get you ready for the next job or open the door to the next opportunity. You have to do it yourself. Second, stay humble, because humility sup-ports lifelong learning. Third, you gotta have hustle.

THE PATH TO HUSTLE:
TAKING CONTROL

Here's the caveat: *I can't teach you hustle.* If you don't have it, if you've never had it, there's nothing I can do for you. (And nobody else can, either.) That may sound harsh, but the brutal truth is, nobody can put in what nature left out. And even if you have it, hustle is hard to sustain throughout your entire career. People sometimes slow down at certain points and then have to get their mojo back later.

So, to keep that fire in your belly, you'll need a plan—you'll need to take control of your career. Here's an obvious analogy: if someone told you that within two years you'd have a heart attack, you'd probably make some big changes immediately. It's a no-brainer, because that kind of prognosis isn't just a wake-up call, it's a "shake-up" call. Nothing is as important as your health.

But what about the health of your career? What if you knew you were going to be fired in a year? Surely you'd make some big changes.

Too often, though, people get complacent. They settle into a rut until one day they wake up and discover that their company has been acquired, their boss has been fired, or they're being downsized. They're out of a job—and out of luck, because they have no idea what to do.

Or they do the opposite. While job-hopping is no longer a negative, they're making leaps without looking. They're bored, they want a change, something pays a little more—so they move. But they never stop to ask: Am I really learning anything?

Whether you're lethargic or you're constantly moving, you need to take control. Think of your career as a long game composed of many short moves. No one is going to do it for you, making sure that you're progressing with each step and job change along the way. It's all on you.

WHAT DRIVES YOU?

Let's be honest here: taking control of your career is hard work—and you're doing it largely on your own. You can't wait for your employer to guide your career development. And if you're making job changes every few years, even if your employer had a development plan for you, you probably aren't staying anywhere long enough for it to take root and pay off.

To keep learning and expanding on your own, you need to be highly motivated. Otherwise, it's too easy to get complacent and coast. The antidote is to be truly energized by what you do.

"Gus" had spent his whole life on the circus crew. For 60-some-odd years, Gus cleaned up after the elephants, a sweaty, dirty job that involved some (pardon the pun) heavy lifting. One day, the circus owner stopped by the elephant yard.

"Gus," he said, "isn't it time you retired?"

"What?" Gus replied with a shocked expression on his face. "And give up show business?"

Every job involves some degree of shoveling you-know-what: the problems, challenges, and difficulties (people and otherwise) that are endemic in any workplace. As a CEO, I can tell you there's as much shoveling at the top as there is at the bottom; it's just different "stuff." Nobody escapes it. The daily grind, though, is really just the dues we all have to pay to do what we truly love—like Gus, shoveling behind the elephants to be part of the show.

So ask yourself: *What motivates me?* Don't say money. Research shows time and again that it really isn't most important. Don't get me wrong, compensation matters, and it must be fair. (We have a whole chapter devoted to how to ask for more money.) But there is so much more to consider than just your current title and salary.

THE THREE COMPONENTS OF MOTIVATION

Motivation has a deeply scientific basis. One of our firm's early thought leaders, the late David McClelland, published seminal books that addressed motivation: *The Achieving Society* (1961),

Human Motivation (1973), and several others. In his breakthrough work, McClelland identified three motivators that have the biggest effect on behavior in the workplace:

ACHIEVEMENT, WHICH HE DEFINED AS THE DESIRE FOR MASTERY AT THE INDIVIDUAL LEVEL;

AFFILIATION, MEANING TO ESTABLISH AND MAINTAIN RELATIONSHIPS; AND

POWER, IN THIS CONTEXT HAVING AN IMPACT OR INFLUENCE.

Which of these three describes you? Does the desire for achievement (mastery) get you out of bed each morning? Is it affiliation (relationships and belonging to a group)? Or is it the desire for power (influence)? You may feel a mix of all three, but one is probably more prominent than the others. Plug into that motivation and find opportunities to experience it in what you do every day. This will increase your engagement as you take control of your career development. (And in the role of a manager, as we'll discuss in Chapter Eight, "Managing for the First Time," knowing which of these components motivates your team members will help you inspire them.)

As you tap into your intrinsic motivators, you'll naturally feel more engaged and inspired. It will show in what you do every day. People will gravitate toward you. Your attitude will lift the altitude of the entire team—or maybe even the entire organization. People will want to engage with you and be part of your team, because let's face it, everybody wants to be around a winner. And you will advance along the career path of your own design.

WHAT GETS YOU UP WITHOUT THE ALARM?

It's 4:30 in the morning, and you're so excited about your job you're up before the alarm. In the darkness before sunrise, you're furiously scrolling through texts, emails, and news on your smartphone as the java brews. If all goes well, you tell yourself, you'll be in the office a good two hours ahead of everyone—not because you're trying to impress the boss, but because you love your job.

Or maybe the alarm isn't set for 4:30 at all. It's more like 6:30, because you can't think of any reason to get up early for, of all things, work! Even then, you aren't out of bed. You hit snooze a half dozen times and roll over, dreading the cheerful looks you'll get from your colleagues later this morning—that is, if you can convince yourself to get up.

So which sounds better?

To take control of career, you need to generate that inner pre-dawn drive—Google-mapping the fastest route to work instead of inventing ways to "legitimately" come in late. And you'll need this sense of hustle day in and day out.

THE SIX STAGES OF CAREER DEVELOPMENT

Even though your career is a string of two- to four-year jobs, it isn't without a plan or purpose. No matter how many times you loop around the labyrinth, you're still headed toward an overarching goal—that is, if you have a map to follow.

While the career journey is different for everyone, there is a master plan that governs just about any journey, as defined by the Six Stages of Career Development.

It's important to calibrate this journey. It isn't a ladder, one job to the next. Rather, you'll travel through various stages of development, spending more time in some than others. You may have one or two jobs in one stage and several jobs in another. You may traverse all six stages, or stop at some intermediate point. It's up to you.

But as a pathway of what's possible, the Six Stages of Career Development can help you keep track of where you've been, where you are, and where you're going.

» *The First Stage: Follower*

At phase one, you are a follower. Typically, this is associated with a first professional job out of college. As a follower, you are action-oriented and task-focused as you carry out what others tell you to do. You will never lead if you don't know how to follow someone!

» *The Second Stage: Collaborator*

Soon you will begin to collaborate with others. You're still operating from your technical skill set, but you begin to develop people skills through collaboration with peers on your team.

» *The Third Stage: Instructor*

As a first-time team leader or manager, you're tapping your people skills when you give instructions to your team, which may comprise only one person. The key here is whether you effectively instruct people on what needs to be done, instead of being the one to do it. Jobs that help you progress at this level include:

Staff Leadership
At this level, you have the responsibility but not the authority. Typical examples include planning projects, installing new systems, troubleshooting problems, negotiating with outside parties, and working in a staff group.

Staff to Line Shifts
This involves moving to a job with an easily determined bottom line or results, managing bigger scope and/or scale, demonstrating new skills/ perspectives, and taking on unfamiliar aspects of your assignments.

» The Fourth Stage: Manager
Your skill set builds as you manage larger teams with bigger goals and objectives. You will need to motivate direct reports and learn how to manage them by giving them objectives and goals, as well as the means to pursue and achieve them. For example, you may be in a "change manager" role—managing a significant effort to change something or implement something of significance, such as total work systems, major new processes and procedures, M&A integration, responses to major competitor initiatives, and reorganizations.

» The Fifth Stage: Influencer
Now things get interesting! At this stage you transition away from directly managing a team to influencing people, especially those who do not directly report to you. Influence is a key leadership skill that you need to develop in order to work with people across the organization, especially those who do not report to you. In fact, you could be influencing people in other departments who are at your level, or even a level above you.

» The Sixth Stage: Leader
At this level, you spend much of your time empowering and inspiring others. As a leader, you don't tell people what to do; rather, you tell them what to think about. Your biggest priority is to motivate people so that they can do more and become more than even they thought possible.

As with any long-term strategy, you'll need to look beyond the needs of the moment to consider a longer time frame, especially the skill development that occurs from job to job. With greater competence and confidence, you can advance to new and unfamiliar terrain on your career journey. This will mean jobs and assignments that best increase your learning, expand your skills, and lead you to the next job.

YOUR INSIDE AND OUTSIDE STRATEGIES

Over the course of your career, you're going to pursue numerous opportunities, both inside and outside your company, and in all kinds of business climates—from strong demand for people with your skills and experience to more difficult times when companies are downsizing and competition is more intense.

But when you take control, it doesn't really matter what's happening "out there." At all times and in all conditions, you must have both inside and outside strategies to keep your career on track.

It comes down to two words: indispensability and insurance. Inside your company, you want to be indispensable, especially to your boss. That buys you job security during downsizing, because you're the last person your boss wants to let go of—you're simply indispensable! On the outside, you have the "insurance" that comes from building relationships in your network and continuously looking outward as you target opportunities elsewhere. When the opportunity is right or when you need to make a move, you're poised and ready. Most importantly, you never make a move because you're panicked. Avoiding those desperate job changes is the number one thing you can do for yourself to keep from derailing your career progress.

> YOU WANT TO BE INDISPENSABLE, ESPECIALLY TO YOUR BOSS. THAT BUYS YOU JOB SECURITY. YOU'RE THE LAST PERSON YOUR BOSS WANTS TO LET GO OF— YOU'RE SIMPLY INDISPENSABLE!

THE INSIDE STRATEGY: INDISPENSABILITY

You need to be the go-to person who gets it done. You're laser-focused on your boss's priorities and the overarching goals of the organization. Here's how:

BUSY DOESN'T CUT IT.

It isn't activity that matters—it's all about accomplishments. Connect your day-to-day activity to how you're addressing the boss's priorities and helping achieve the team's and the company's goals.

MOVE THE NEEDLE.

Measurement matters. If you're in sales, you're probably being held accountable for quotas and similar metrics. But even if you're in IT, finance, marketing, HR, or other functions, you can (and should) connect the dots between what you do every day and moving the needle toward the company's objectives.

FOCUS ON WHAT ISN'T BEING DONE.

Look for what is not currently being done and take it on. You'll go a long way to proving your indispensability and your ability to take on more responsibilities should the workforce shrink. But keep in mind that there will be times when this will increase your burden. For example, during the last recession, it wasn't uncommon for one person to be doing the work of two or three. Those who took on that responsibility without complaining

positioned themselves for career growth as things improved. Are you willing to do that?

GET ON THE RIGHT TEAM.

Companies often lean more heavily on certain strategies than others to generate growth and/or increase profitability. Volunteer for task forces and projects that increase your knowledge and exposure. The more you can align yourself—directly or indirectly—with those key initiatives now, the better positioned you'll be later.

ACT LIKE YOU ALREADY HAVE THE NEXT JOB.

One way to advance within your current organization is to act like you're already at the next level. In fact, when you officially get the title and the bigger scope of responsibilities, people shouldn't be surprised. The best compliment you can receive on your promotion is, "Oh, I thought you were already at that level." Show that you're comfortable working with people several levels above you. Earn the respect of not only your boss but also your boss's boss. Think substance! If you see a problem, own it and address it. With more experience, you can even anticipate problems before they arise.

THE OUTSIDE STRATEGY: HAVING "INSURANCE"

Even as you implement your inside strategy to become indispensable, you need to look externally as well. There will be times when the next best move is with another employer. You may even change industries or take on a new role in order to expand your skill sets and experience.

There are also times when your outside strategy acts as a contingency plan in case things happen that are beyond your control. For example, your boss may leave (or be fired), or your department may be reduced, outsourced, or eliminated. If that happens, you're going to need a rip cord to pull externally so you can land on your feet. To give yourself a sense of urgency, ask yourself: What would you do if you knew you were being let go in six months?

In every circumstance and business climate, you need to have "insurance" to give yourself the maximum opportunities.

TARGET OPPORTUNITIES.

Start now to identify opportunities outside your company by targeting. Make a list of the industries that fit your background and skill set. What companies interest you most? Do you admire their mission and purpose, and can you see yourself working there? What geographic areas appeal to you?

BUILD RELATIONSHIPS.

Notice I did not say "network." Before you can network—i.e., approach people for help getting a job or to inquire about a job opening in their company—you need to build a strong network through relationships. Do things that others find valuable, such as acting as a sounding board,

providing help or advice, or passing along an interesting article.

LOSE THE RESUME.

Yes, you do need an up-to-date resume. But don't expect it to be more than 10 percent of what it takes to get a new job (not the 90 percent that people assume).

Instead, focus on the story you tell about yourself, your purpose and passion, and your accomplishments. Get in the habit of presenting yourself this way as you build relationships and network with people, both inside and outside the company.

THE BRUTAL TRUTH

Be honest: As you read this advice, did you automatically think "I do that … and that … and that one too"? Really? If you do, then you probably are advancing regularly in your career. If that's not happening, then you might want to reconsider what's really your truth.

The problem is, people lie all the time, especially to themselves. They convince themselves that they're go-getters, but the truth is that the last thing they went out and got was probably lunch. They're complacent, walking around in a state of comfortable numbness. They think that time in a chair and doing a "decent job" will eventually get them noticed. The phone will ring, and a new job will await them—like they've won the lottery or one of those radio call-in contests.

That's not how it works. If you don't wake up to this brutal honesty with yourself then you don't have hustle. You'll just keep hitting the snooze button on your career (and probably, literally, every morning). But it doesn't have to be that way. You can become more engaged and motivated to perform at a consistently high level that leads to advancement.

THE FOUR CAREER KNOCKOUT PUNCHES

Finally, as your career path progresses, you'll need to develop in four key areas. Each is so important to your advancement, I call them "knockout punches." Possess them, and you'll be a knockout in any job. Fail to develop them, and you'll be knocked out by the competition.

You can use these knockout punches as a guide to point you in the direction of specific opportunities that will help you develop each of them. Like the Six Stages of Career Development, these "punches" are the longer-term view of how to take control and advance to where you want to be next.

1 **A global mindset.**
You will be required to show some global experience, such as an international assignment or, at a minimum, work on a global team that requires significant travel to operations or clients abroad. (See Chapter Thirteen, "Going Global," to help you.) You must develop a global mindset if you want to compete in a marketplace that is both borderless and heavily influenced by local nuance. You'll deal with different languages, cultural norms, and business rules, which will provide you with opportunities to grow and stretch. You'll develop cross-cultural agility, enabling you to work with and relate to people across multiple cultures.

2 **Dealing with ambiguity.**
You must be comfortable with ambiguity. In fact, studies show that 90 percent of the problems confronting managers and people in higher positions are ambiguous—neither the problem nor the solution is clear. Dealing with ambiguity means making good decisions based on the information you have at the time. If you can deal with ambiguity, you can effectively cope

with change, decide and act without knowing the total picture, shift gears comfortably, and handle risk and uncertainty.

3 Handling and managing change.

Organizations today are dealing with unprecedented levels of change. Consider the rapid advancements in technology: artificial intelligence and machine learning, the Internet of Things, and the disintermediation that continues to disrupt industries. Being comfortable with change means not only reacting to it, but also being a catalyst for it. You must demonstrate the ability to handle and manage change by putting new ideas into practice and being highly interested in continuous improvement. You are cool under pressure and can handle the heat and consequences of being on the front line of change.

4 Mastering a faster pace.

Along with widespread change, businesses are experiencing a faster pace of play. Everything from product cycles to time to market is being compressed, so you must be able to handle the faster pace. You know how to encourage others to work smarter and use technology to their advantage, but you don't push the organization at a pace faster than it can handle.

These aren't check-the-box competencies; they take time to master. But if you take control of your journey, you will ensure that you gain these experiences, as they will be essential to your growth.

YOUR 5 TAKEAWAYS

FOR TAKING CONTROL

Find your inner hustle. Call it fire in the belly, or drive. It is the sustaining energy that keeps you moving, especially when the going gets tough. With hustle, you'll recognize those difficult times as opportunities to challenge yourself, learn, and grow.

Know what motivates you (and it isn't money). The science of human behavior tells us that achievement (mastery), affiliation (relationships and belonging), and power (influence) are powerful, deep-seated motivations. Connecting with your motivation will enhance your engagement.

Navigate by the Six Stages of Career Development. Each stage acts as a point along the map outlining a long journey. You will spend more time in some stages than others. You may not get to all six. But being aware of each stage, you'll have a general road map to follow on your sojourn.

Have an inside and an outside strategy. Over

CONTINUED

the course of your career, you're going to pursue numerous opportunities, both inside and outside your company. With strategies for both, you'll become indispensable to your current boss and position yourself to advance within your current employer—while gaining "insurance" in case you have to or want to make a move to a new external opportunity.

Focus on the four "knockout punches." You must have these key "punches"—a global mindset, dealing with ambiguity, handling and managing change, and mastering a faster pace—in your arsenal if you want to advance. Each skill is developed and practiced over time, as you gain experience and expertise.

Chapter Two

UNCOVERING YOUR BLIND SPOTS:

Are You Self-Aware?

The lecture hall was nearly full, and every eye was trained in my direction. At the end of my presentation on career development at this prestigious university, a young man in the back row called out, "What's the one thing I need to know so I can get *your* job one day?" He sat, arms folded, his baseball cap on backward.

"There is one important quality," I replied. "It's so important, in fact, it's the foundation for your career development."

Now I had their attention.

When I asked the students what they thought that secret ingredient was, they came up with the predictable list: their intelligence, their digital savvy, their connections—plus the fact that they were attending one of the best schools in the country. Not one of them guessed the real answer.

"Whether you're trying to get a job or keep a job, it comes down to the same: self-awareness," I told them. "You can't go through life thinking you're this when you're really that. You can't pretend to be a lion if you're only a squirrel."

Self-awareness is everything—and it's a concept you're going to read about not only in this chapter but throughout this book. If you aren't self-aware, you'll never learn, never grow, and definitely never improve. You'll ignore your blind spots, overestimate your strengths, and gloss over your weaknesses. And that is a recipe for derailing your career.

The cost of self-delusion is high. Research shows that people who greatly overstate their abilities are 6.2 times more likely to derail than those who have accurate self-awareness. If that isn't a case for becoming more self-aware, I don't know what is.

Q Nobody can be good at everything. So shouldn't I just focus on my strengths—my talents and what I do best?

A The problem with that approach is that people almost always overestimate their strengths. They think they're far better at something than they really are. And they have blind spots that, no matter how glaring, they just can't (or won't) see. The truth is, no matter how strong your strengths are, your blind spots can absolutely derail you.

I once engaged my senior team from all over the world in a live assessment of my leadership strengths and blind spots. I gathered them to rate me using remote-control "clickers" to ensure anonymity. I brought in a facilitator who was a former hostage negotiator—this person clearly could handle high-pressure situations.

After each question, the clicker results immediately displayed on a huge screen at the front of the room. It was intense, to say the least. As insightful and appreciated as the feedback was, that wasn't the only purpose of this exercise. My intention was to demonstrate a willingness to be vulnerable and humble, which are precursors to being self-aware.

I put myself on the spot in order to model for my team the vulnerability of being willing to "look in the mirror"—in this case, publicly and transparently. That's why, at the end of the three-hour session, I

PEOPLE WHO OVERSTATE THEIR ABILITIES ARE 6.2 TIMES MORE LIKELY TO DERAIL.

gave each person a small mirror as a reminder that a leader can only inspire and motivate others if he or she is willing to undertake an honest self-assessment. Only by looking in the mirror can you lead yourself, before you lead others.

So if you're serious about taking control and advancing in your career, you need to be **AWARE:**

A → Avoid the "brick wall"
W → Wake up to your blind spots
A → Assess your traits and drivers
R → Rate your competencies
E → Express your experiences

A → AVOID THE "BRICK WALL"

Let's say you're a rising star—not only a high performer but also high potential. Your boss notices this, along with your eagerness to take on bigger assignments. So you get more responsibility.

Then—suddenly, dramatically—you hit a wall. You can't keep up. Deadlines are missed. You "lose it" in team meetings. You start to blame others. You're arrogant and ignore feedback. People don't want to work for you.

This is classic *career derailment*. And if you're like most people, until you crash and burn you won't even know what hit you. The reason? Missing the first "A" in **AWARE**: you failed to notice the brick wall that was looming in front of you.

It's not that you've lost all your potential, it's that something bigger and more corrosive got in the way. And it isn't just about the obvious few missed deadlines or product launch gone awry. It's far deeper than that. You have serious blind spots about how you act, interact, and get work done that led you straight into that wall.

As you'll read in this chapter, all of us have traits, drivers, and competencies. Along with our experiences, these components are what Korn Ferry calls the "Four Dimensions" (4D for short) that define talent.

Four Dimensions
That Define Talent

TRAITS: your behaviors, natural tendencies, and abilities

DRIVERS: your motivations, values, and what's important to you

COMPETENCIES: what you're proficient at

EXPERIENCES: the sum total of your accomplishments

The 4D (which you'll assess for yourself later in this chapter) reveal not only what you're good at but also those blind spots that can derail you. This is "mirror, mirror" time, and you need the unvarnished truth. *Everyone* has blind spots. Everyone needs feedback to grow.

Based on our work with very talented and high-potential people at all levels, here are the most common derailers:

Bricks in the Wall:
The Dirty Dozen Career Derailers

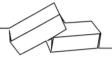

1 → **UNAWARENESS.** You can't see yourself as you are; overestimate your strengths and underestimate your weaknesses; lack self-knowledge.

2 → **RIGIDITY.** You resist change; struggle outside your comfort zone; have real difficulty adapting to new things, whether a boss, process, technology, or strategy.

3 → **DISORGANIZATION.** You let things fall through the cracks; overcommit and underdeliver; drop the ball on key details; are seen as unreliable.

4 → **ARROGANCE.** You always think you're right; dismiss others' input and ideas; make others feel inferior; are detached.

5 → **UNTRUSTWORTHINESS.** You say one thing and do another; break confidences; gossip about others.

6 → **CRACKING UNDER PRESSURE.** You can't handle pressure and stress; are emotional and unpredictable—even getting hostile toward others; have lower performance when things get tough.

7 → **DEFENSIVENESS.** You can't take criticism and negative feedback; deny mistakes and faults; blame others—and the messenger.

8 → **NOT BEING A TEAM PLAYER.** You don't pull together with others; don't share credit for successes; you undermine team spirit.

9 → **HEARING, BUT NOT LISTENING.** You hear, but you don't really listen; are insensitive—unaware of or unfeeling about the impact of what you say and do to others; have poor interpersonal skills and never ask about others.

10 → **POOR PERFORMANCE.** You're inconsistent in hitting targets and objectives; can't produce results across a variety of challenges; procrastinate; lack experience and expertise.

11 → **LACK OF INDEPENDENCE.** You stay with the same boss or mentor for too long; have difficulty handling tough assignments without help.

12 → **OVERRELIANCE ON ONE SKILL.** You are a "one-trick pony," using the same core talent, function, or technology; act as if one talent alone is sufficient.

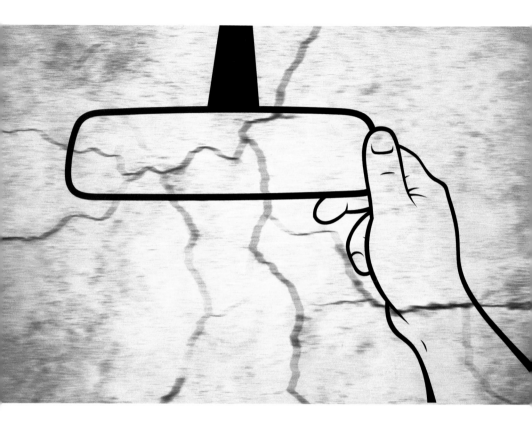

W → WAKE UP
TO YOUR BLIND SPOTS

If **you want to avoid hitting the wall** at some point in your career, you need a big dose of self-awareness to see where you are lacking or have gaps in your development. This brings us to the "W" in **AWARE:** wake up to your blind spots.

Some years ago, I met "Pamela," a marketing leader who was devising and directing the strategy for a retail chain and really making an impact on the company. Not only was she a highly capable chief marketing officer, but she was also among a half-dozen candidates from across the company who were being groomed as possible successors to the CEO within the next five years.

While Pamela had definite strengths, particularly related to her current position, she had a few weaknesses. For example, she knew she wasn't as strong in financial acumen as she'd need to be as CEO. So when the company wanted the leading succession candidates to be assessed against the requirements of the CEO position, Pamela embraced the process.

Pamela got more than she bargained for. That deficit in financial acumen showed up, as expected. But there was other feedback, and it hit hard. The assessment showed blind spots when it came to important areas for advancing her career, such as having a global perspective, engaging and inspiring others, and tolerating ambiguity. It was a sobering truth, but Pamela took it all in. If she wanted to reach the pinnacle in her career, she needed to address those blind spots.

The day after she received the tough feedback, Pamela emailed the Korn Ferry assessment team: "I'm back in the office today, and I'm already working on my development areas." Within a week, she had a plan to get three stretch assignments from the CEO, and she was seeking bimonthly feedback. To solidify her commitment, she hired a coach to work with her. Today, she is the CEO of a Fortune 1000 company.

Although that's obviously a great outcome, don't mistake that as the moral of the story. It isn't about having the best assessment—it's what you do with that information. Pamela woke up to her blind spots and did something about them. And you need to do the same, using the assessments you'll find throughout this chapter (and now also on *KFAdvance.com*).

A → ASSESS YOUR TRAITS AND DRIVERS

Now we really get into it—the second "A" in **AWARE:** assess your traits and drivers. Traits are the core, hardwired parts of your makeup. Some traits can be developed, but most are inborn. They define who you are. Drivers, meanwhile, are what motivate you—your passion and purpose. Together, they compose who you are.

YOUR TRAITS— NATURAL TENDENCIES AND ABILITIES

Traits are largely what you're born with. They include your personality traits and intellectual capacity. Traits guide your behavior, but at times they can be difficult to observe, which is why assessments are so important. Traits not only affect how you perform in your current job, they also put the spotlight on what you need to advance.

Traits can change slowly over time as you take on new challenges. For example, with practice and even some coaching, an introvert can become more outgoing and comfortable speaking with others.

Here are some common traits and how they are defined in a business context.

ADAPTABILITY: Comfortable with unanticipated changes of direction or approach. Those who are highly adaptable are willing and able to nimbly change, adapt easily to changes in situations, adjust to constraints, and manage or rebound from adversity.

ASSERTIVENESS: Able to take charge and direct others. People who are assertive tend to be seen as aggressive and decisive.

CURIOSITY: Can tackle problems in a novel way, sees patterns in complex information, and pursues deep understanding. Those who are very curious enjoy solving complex problems with creative solutions and addressing issues in thoughtful and intellectually driven ways.

FOCUS: Has a preference for organization, procedure, and exactitude. Those who are highly focused demand structure and tend to be seen as systematic, detail oriented, and in control.

NEED FOR ACHIEVEMENT: Motivated by work or activities that allow your skills and abilities to be tested against external standards. Those with a high need for achievement appreciate working hard, judge their own achievements according to their goals, and strive to meet and exceed standards.

PERSISTENCE: Passionate and steadfast in pursuit of personally valued long-term or lifetime goals, despite obstacles, discouragement, or distraction. Highly persistent people push through obstacles and do not give up on difficult tasks.

RISK-TAKING: Willing to take a risk or a stand. Those who are comfortable with risk-taking may prefer success over security and exhibit a willingness to take substantial risk when making decisions.

TOLERANCE OF AMBIGUITY: Comfortable with uncertain, vague, or contradictory information. People who can handle ambiguity are energized by these situations, are open to alternative solutions, and can work productively despite not having a clear view of the future.

TO GET AN IN-DEPTH LOOK AT YOUR TRAITS, HERE IS A SHORT ASSESSMENT DERIVED FROM KORN FERRY'S EXTENSIVE INTELLECTUAL PROPERTY.

Know Yourself   Your KF4D Assessments

4 POINTS
Strongly Disagree ▶

3 POINTS
Disagree ▶

2 POINTS
Agree ▶

1 POINT
Strongly Agree ▶

1 POINT
Strongly Disagree ▶

2 POINTS
Disagree ▶

3 POINTS
Agree ▶

4 POINTS
Strongly Agree ▶

Assessing Your Traits

1   I understand people's feelings and motives.   [   ]

2   I focus on the future or past more than the present.   [   ]

3   I strive to achieve lofty goals.   [   ]

4   What happens to me depends mostly on my own efforts.   [   ]

5   I tend to seek out people who think the way I do.   [   ]

6   I tend to give people the benefit of the doubt.   [   ]

7   New ideas take me off course.   [   ]

8   I prefer independent work.   [   ]

9   I am known for motivating others.   [   ]

10   I generally expect things to turn out for the best.   [   ]

11   I'd rather not be in charge.   [   ]

12   My work suffers when I am stressed.   [   ]

45

PRESENCE
Add items 1, 9, and 11 and refer to the descriptions below.

1 to 6 points
Your pattern of scores indicates a predisposition toward rationality, leading by example, and deferring to others for direction. These characteristics are hallmarks of the "vital many" in organizations, and are sometimes associated with jobs whose tasks are repeatable, structured, and predictable. Interestingly, individuals working in administrative services, accounting, and manufacturing often show a similar pattern of scores.

7 to 12 points
Your pattern of scores indicates a predisposition toward social and emotional presence. You are likely to be viewed as sociable, persuasive, commanding, and poised. These characteristics are hallmarks of organizational leaders and high-level managers, and are typically associated with jobs whose tasks are novel and unpredictable and involve people management. Similar scores are often seen among individuals in communications, sales, marketing, retail, and executive management.

AGREEABLENESS
Add items 5, 6, and 8 and refer to the descriptions below.

1 to 6 points
Your pattern of scores indicates a predisposition toward skepticism, social caution, and independence. Your preference for solo efforts may sometimes present challenges to promotion, but can be an advantage for roles that require limited or only prescriptive collaboration. Similar patterns of scores are typically seen among individuals working in public safety, manufacturing, and legal and administrative services.

7 to 12 points
Your pattern of scores indicates a tendency to be considerate, humble, collaborative, and inclusive, and to see people as generally trustworthy. These characteristics are key to positive teamwork outcomes and are often strongly sought after by employers. Similar results are often seen for individuals working in human resources, marketing, consulting, research and development, and executive management.

STRIVING
Add items 3, 4, and 7 and refer to the descriptions below.

1 to 6 points
Your pattern of scores indicates an aversion to competition, a tendency to be opportunistic, and a predisposition toward believing that fate, luck, or uncontrollable forces play a large role in determining life outcomes. In general, this pattern is sometimes associated with increased creativity, but is not typical of upper-level managers and can create challenges to job satisfaction and commitment in any role. Similar patterns are often seen among individuals working in communications, customer service, administrative services, and especially creative roles.

7 to 12 points
Your pattern of scores indicates a predisposition toward achievement orientation, reliability, and persistence. You are likely to be viewed as hard-working, results driven, and dependable. You likely persist in the face of obstacles when pursuing goals. These characteristics are a key to success in any role and are seen at high levels among successful incumbents across the management pipeline. Similar scores are typically seen in individuals working in executive-management roles, strategic planning, legal, marketing, and healthcare.

POSITIVITY
Add items 2, 10, and 12 and refer to the descriptions below.

1 to 6 points
Your pattern of scores indicates a predisposition toward realism, emotional transparency, and rumination. A tendency to dwell on the past or future can be a key to learning from experience, but is also sometimes associated with elevated stress and anxiety. However, people may find it easy to know your mood, which can be refreshing and is sometimes needed in communication. Similar scores are often seen among individuals working in manufacturing, creative fields, communications, and sales.

7 to 12 points
Your pattern of scores indicates a tendency toward positivity, optimism, composure, and mindfulness. You may have a tendency to reserve judgment and "live in the moment," which can serve as a protection against stress and anxiety. Similar score patterns are typically seen among individuals working in public safety, healthcare, retail, and executive management.

DRIVERS: WHAT MOTIVATES YOU

Drivers can be very specific or very broad. They also can fluctuate based on your circumstances or stage in life. At every stage, they are crucial to where you will fit best—in what kind of company culture and environment and working for what kind of boss. And they'll tell you how likely you are to be engaged by your job.

When you know what drives you, your career advancement follows a more definitive path. It's easier to find an organization that is aligned with your purpose. In the same way, when organizations understand what drives people, they find it easier to connect with them—to understand what makes them tick and tap into their energy. If there's a mismatch between a person's drivers and the organizational culture, that's bad news for all involved.

Signs That You've Checked Out

✔ Thursdays are the new Fridays, and Fridays the new Saturdays—and Mondays…well, enough said.

✔ When you are out of the office, you set up an automatic response that states "I will have no access to email…" Like where, Mars?

✔ You wish your commute were longer.

✔ You welcome really long calls from your in-laws.

✔ Your desk is a great place to nap.

✔ Your lunch hour typically ends with you saying, "Oh shoot—I had a 3:30 meeting."

✔ You keep beating your personal best in Candy Crush… at work.

Your drivers or motivators lie at the heart of critical questions: What's most important to you? What do you find rewarding? Most significantly, your drivers factor into culture fit, engagement, and performance. Here are some drivers and how they affect motivation and performance in the workplace. (Again, be sure to take the assessment that follows here or on *KFAdvance.com*.)

BALANCE: The motivation to achieve a balance between work and personal life. Those who score high in this area prefer work-related flexibility and broadly defined self-development, and they avoid high-stress, life-defining job roles.

CHALLENGE: The motivation to achieve in the face of tough obstacles. Those with this motivation prefer challenging and competitive work assignments and environments that often preclude them from operating comfortably and in familiar ways.

COLLABORATION: The preference to work interdependently, to make decisions, and pursue goals in a group. Those who are highly collaborative prefer to be part of teams, to build consensus, share responsibility, and use social behaviors to achieve work-related success.

INDEPENDENCE: The preference for independence and an entrepreneurial approach. Those who desire independence prefer freedom from organizational constraints and want to set and pursue their own vision. They also value employability over job security.

POWER: The desire to achieve work-related status and influence, and to make an impact on the organization. Those who seek power desire visibility and responsibility within an organization, and they want to acquire a high degree of influence.

STRUCTURE: The preference for work-related stability, predictability, and structure. Those with this preference value job security, familiar problems and solutions, and jobs that often require depth and specialized knowledge or skill.

Know Yourself

Your KF4D Assessments

Add items 1, 4, 5, 7, 8, and 9 to calculate your promotion-focused score

Add items 2, 3, 6, 10, 11, and 12 to calculate your preservation-focused score

1 POINT ▶
Very Little

2 POINTS ▶
Little

3 POINTS ▶
Some

4 POINTS ▶
Very Much

Compare your promotion-focused and preservation-focused scores to see which is higher. Then read the description of the higher driver for insights from similar responders.

Assessing Your Drivers

How much are you motivated by…

1 Developing and pursuing your own vision [   ]

2 Working with others toward a common goal [   ]

3 Achieving a balanced and multifaceted lifestyle [   ]

4 Gaining the respect and recognition of others [   ]

5 Winning against tough competition [   ]

6 Predictability and stability [   ]

7 Freedom from organizational constraints [   ]

8 Influence and power [   ]

9 New and challenging assignments [   ]

10 Traditions and consistency [   ]

11 Belonging and acceptance in a group [   ]

12 Work-life balance [   ]

PROMOTION-FOCUSED DESCRIPTION

Your pattern of scores indicates promotion-focused motivational tendencies. This means that in work you typically strive to approach desired circumstances, rather than avoid undesired circumstances. You are likely to experience eagerness with goal striving and joy with goal attainment. Individuals who are promotion focused tend to prefer challenging roles that allow opportunity for personal growth, upward mobility, and achievement. They may pursue the respect and recognition of others and/or tend toward an entrepreneurial spirit and approach to work, while preferring environments in which promotion and rewards are granted according to merit. Individuals working in creative roles are among the highest scorers on promotion-focused motives. Other high scorers often include executive managers, sales people, strategic planners, and financial-services professionals.

PRESERVATION-FOCUSED DESCRIPTION

Your pattern of scores indicates preservation-focused motivational tendencies. This means that in work you typically strive to avoid undesired circumstances, rather than approach and strive for desired circumstances. Individuals who are preservation focused tend to strive for stability, reliability, and if possible, low stress at work. They are motivated by job security, achieving a well-rounded background lifestyle, structured well-defined roles, and being part of a supportive group. They typically prefer jobs in which promotion and reward come via seniority and/or tenure. Individuals working in healthcare are among the highest scorers on preservation-focused motives. Other high scorers often include educators, lawyers, and people working in research and development and engineering.

R → RATE YOUR COMPETENCIES

Now that you have a better understanding of who you are (your traits and drivers), you can take a deeper dive into what you do. This brings us to the "R" in **AWARE:** rate your competencies—those skills and abilities you possess that are essential for advancing in your career and achieving success.

What makes you successful? It's a straightforward question, yet most people can't answer it. They fumble around, describing what they've done or reciting their job description. But they have no idea what their competencies are, because they don't understand the concept.

Your competencies may include some natural talent. But many competencies are intentionally developed over time and built up as part of a particular job assignment. Functional and technical skills are also part of your competencies. For example, if you're in finance, then having strong financial acumen is a big part of your competency. Some competencies are harder to develop than others, but with the right motivation and support (coaching, stretch assignments, feedback) nearly everyone can make measurable progress on competencies.

Know Yourself — Your KF4D Assessments

Assessing Your Competencies

1 POINT ▶
No Skill

2 POINTS ▶
Low Skill

3 POINTS ▶
Skilled

4 POINTS ▶
Very Skilled

1   Managing conflicts   [   ]

2   Having a broad perspective   [   ]

3   Understanding the business   [   ]

4   Ensuring accountability in yourself and others   [   ]

5   Staying engaged when things are unclear   [   ]

6   Addressing the needs of multiple stakeholders   [   ]

7   Making and executing plans   [   ]

8   Inspiring others   [   ]

9   Collaborating   [   ]

10   Leading yourself and others through a crisis   [   ]

11   Communicating effectively to diverse audiences   [   ]

12   Building effective teams   [   ]

13   Developing your skills, knowledge, and abilities   [   ]

14   Delegating and removing obstacles to get work done   [   ]

PEOPLE COMPETENCIES

Add items 1, 8, 9, 11, and 12 and refer to the descriptions below.

High Score ≥15 / High scorers on people competencies use communication skills along with interpersonal and organizational savvy to develop talent and navigate through organizations. High scores are notably associated with increased promotion likelihood and better performance in most roles. Job functions such as executive management, customer/client service, marketing, sales, and even information technology all tend to have individuals with elevated people competencies.

Low Score <15 / Low scorers on people competencies tend to prefer and do better working independently and in task-oriented ways. Technical and process-oriented roles are more common among low scorers. Without strong people competencies, promotion can be difficult, as can performance in many of today's organizations, which increasingly rely on collaboration, group efforts, and leadership via lateral influence. Lower scores are typically seen among accountants and administrative-services professionals.

THOUGHT COMPETENCIES

Add items 2, 3, and 6 and refer to the descriptions below.

High Score ≥9 / High scorers on thought competencies tend to combine business insight with broad and strategic thinking in ways that help them manage and deal with complexity. They tend toward innovation and well-informed organization-related decision-making. As with people competencies, high scores in thought competencies are notably associated with increased promotion likelihood and better performance in most roles. Job functions such as executive management, strategic planning, financial services, marketing, research and development, and information technology all tend to be occupied by individuals with elevated thought competencies.

Low Score <9 / Low scorers on thought competencies tend to have a narrow perspective on work and organizational outcomes. They prefer tried-and-true methods and structured work environments with more rote tasks and less complexity. Without strong thought competencies, promotion can be difficult, as can performance in many of today's organizations, which are increasingly complex, fast paced, and change-oriented.

RESULTS COMPETENCIES

Add items 4, 7, and 14 and refer to the descriptions below.

High Score ≥9 / High scorers on results competencies tend to combine action orientation, resourcefulness, and effective planning to drive execution and results. They tend to value and demonstrate hard work and accountability in themselves and others. While high scores are markedly associated with increased promotion likelihood and better performance in virtually all roles, related skills are relatively easy to develop in many cases. Job functions such as executive management, strategic planning, sales, manufacturing, and operations tend to be occupied by individuals with notably elevated results competencies.

Low Score <9 / Low scorers on results competencies tend to have a steady, unfocused and deferential approach to work. They defer to others to make plans, to ensure execution, and to maintain accountability within the organization. They may seem content or even complacent, are not driven by competition or high standards, and don't place value on exceeding expectations. Without strong results competencies, both promotion and performance can be difficult in most roles.

SELF-COMPETENCIES

Add items 5, 10, and 13 and refer to the descriptions below.

High Score ≥9 / High scorers on self-competencies tend to combine fast learning with resilience in ways that help them make the most of their experiences, including successes and failures. They tend to be adaptable and courageous, and able to manage and navigate ambiguous circumstances. High scores are markedly associated with increased promotion likelihood and better performance in most roles. Unlike results competencies, however, many key self-competencies are scarce and relatively hard to develop. Job functions such as executive management, strategic planning, and creative roles tend to be occupied by individuals with notably elevated self-competencies.

Low Score <9 / Low scorers on self-competencies tend to have an inflexible and process-oriented approach to work, while preferring roles that are well structured, detail-oriented, and predictable. They may not learn effectively from experiences, especially failures, and may fail to adapt to changing or diverse circumstances. They may lack resilience and fail in crisis situations. Without strong self-competencies, promotion can be difficult, as can performance in many of today's organizations, which are increasingly complex and change-oriented, and characterized by periods of ambiguity in goals and solutions.

E → EXPRESS YOUR EXPERIENCES

Now we come to the "E" in **AWARE:** express your experiences, which along with competencies are part of "what you do." There's no surprise here. Your experiences are what you've done—the bullet points on your resume. But it doesn't stop there. What most people don't fully appreciate is what experiences can do: they help you define the story you tell.

Experiences transcend job titles. It's all about accomplishments—the story you tell about yourself, whether you're networking with someone or interviewing for a new position, internal or external. Your experiences are the narrative of your career progression that allows people to get to know you. Don't go on and on about all your activities, instead of focusing on your accomplishments. (You'll make people wonder: Do you have any?)

YOUR EXPERIENCES ARE THE NARRATIVE OF YOUR CAREER PROGRESSION.

Amassing experiences is akin to strength training at the gym. The weight and number of repetitions both matter. Heavyweight jobs are those that include high visibility, a risk of failure, ambiguity, and a broad scope of responsibility. The more difficult and perspective broadening the experience, the faster it bulks up muscle. It's ongoing—upward and outward. This is not a "one and done" process to get to the next job. It's the long game played throughout your career.

The fundamental tools to guide you are here in this chapter. This is the "rinse and repeat" of continuously becoming more self-aware, uncovering blind spots (you will always have areas you need to develop), honing your traits, identifying your drivers, and building new competencies. It's a lifelong process.

If you keep working on yourself, you will build a firm foundation for the rest of your career. But if you don't, then what you're building, by default, is that brick wall you're going to hit at some point. The choice is yours.

The pages that follow offer advice, guidance, and real-world perspective on numerous areas that can help you take control and advance your career. Many of these areas are skill based, and most have to do with how you work and interact with others. But these upcoming chapters by themselves will not be effective if you don't do this work first, starting with becoming highly self-aware.

YOUR 5 TAKEAWAYS

FOR BECOMING
SELF-AWARE

Self-awareness is self-improvement—the ability to see yourself clearly and honestly. It's the truth about who you are and what you do.

Without knowing your blind spots, you're vulnerable to hit a brick wall in your career—no matter how talented and high potential you are.

Feedback and information about your strengths and weaknesses are only a start; what matters most is what you do with that input.

Assess, assess, assess. You can't see yourself clearly if you only assume. You need to have the courage to truly look at yourself.

Define the story you can tell about yourself—who you are, what you do, what motivates you, and what you've accomplished.

Chapter Three

MAKING MORE MONEY:

Accepting No, Getting to Yes

Whenever I give a speech, I know there's one sure way to get everyone's attention: talk about money. I'll ask, "How many of you think you are underpaid or overpaid? Can we have a show of hands, please?" I've yet to see anyone raise their hand for being overpaid.

And yet very rarely do people do anything about it. There is a stigma—a massive corporate taboo—around asking for more money. I get it, the "money conversation" is downright awkward. Money is a high-anxiety topic everyone hates; it's emotionally charged. In relationships, money is one of the main reasons couples fight, more than in-laws or who should take the garbage out. In the workplace, it's just as problematic. No one knows how to engage in the money conversation. First, most people try an indirect approach. It always starts out the same way: "It's not really about the money ..." Really? Of course it's about the money! But people are so uncomfortable talking about money that they'd rather avoid discussing it directly.

Or when people do ask for a raise, the way they go about it makes you wonder if they really want it—or whether they've thought about a raise strategy. Seriously, it's sad how many folks work so hard to actually deserve a raise, then totally blow the way they go about asking for it. Many will just blurt it out during a meeting with a manager or back into the topic in a way that turns off the boss before they've even started. As for doing research, I can't remember the last time I heard about someone checking out the market rate for their job before asking for a raise—

Q Given my workload and what I've accomplished, I feel I really deserve a raise—and more than the 2 percent I got last year. How can I ask for a raise in a way that won't upset my boss and ruin our working relationship?

A The "money conversation" isn't one and done. It should be part of ongoing conversations about goals and deliverables. But the short answer is to prepare! Write down your best case for receiving a raise in terms that will be most meaningful to your boss. It isn't about the money you want—it's the value you bring.

or tried to get some insight into what their boss or boss's boss might be thinking at the time.

In fact, the problem is so widespread it's easy to categorize these requests into a handful of characters. What's interesting is how differently each one goes about asking for money, but they all end up in the same unhappy place.

INDIRECT IRENE sends the boss an email that hints about wanting to discuss something. Or she leaves a voicemail: "I, uh, want to know if we can, uh, talk about something around, you know, my last raise ... Not urgent. When you have time." Now try to imagine being on the receiving end of that request. You know full well she hasn't thought about how the conversation is supposed to go. So nothing happens.

OUTTA-HERE OLLIE is just the opposite, being quite direct—only in the worst ways. He wakes up one morning and decides that today is the day. With two kids in college, a mortgage, and car payments, he needs more money, and this sense of panic forces him to act rashly. He marches into the boss's office with an attitude of "if I don't get a raise, I'm outta here." That day, HR starts a search to find his replacement. Ollie was indeed outta there.

RESENTFUL RENEE neither complains nor says thank you when she gets a cost-of-living increase. Yet inside her is a soul burning with anger. She knows she's getting what everyone gets, but even though she can't quite prove why, she believes she deserves more. And in her mind, someday the world will wake up and realize her value. Until then, she will take her pay quietly and refuse to do any extra work whatsoever—which of course only guarantees the same cost-of-living increase the following year.

PASSIVE-AGGRESSIVE PAUL doesn't hesitate to complain to any of his colleagues who will listen that his pay is way off. He has no idea how much others are actually earning but tries to spread his negativity around because misery loves company. Few, if any, bite. Nevertheless, PAP tells his boss he hears others are unhappy about their pay. The boss sees right through it.

LYING LARRY tries the oldest trick in the book, trying to force his boss's hand by claiming to have another job offer with a significant raise in salary. (There is a strategy around this when you really do have another offer—read on—but Larry only fabricated his.) When the boss asks to see the offer letter (I typically do this, and so do other companies), Larry has nothing to show.

There's absolutely nothing wrong with asking for more money—so long as it's done the right way. Asking for money won't be a blemish on your reputation. You can be the squeaky wheel who gets the boss's attention. But it's important to realize that this is a serious endeavor and should never be rushed or done impulsively. Most people, however, want what they want when they want it. When it comes to getting a bigger paycheck, they can't figure out why the boss isn't delivering. They think the boss is just being stingy. The fact is, your boss simply isn't thinking about you and your paycheck as much as you are. More money does not come on demand.

How to Ask for More

M → Meet face-to-face with your boss

O → Own your performance objectives

R → Research your "worth"

E → Envision your endgame

If you get the raise—congratulations!

If not, get clarity from your boss on what you must deliver to earn the raise you want.

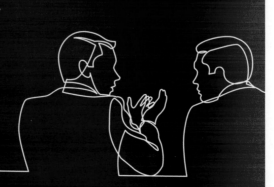

RAISING THE MONEY ISSUE

If you really want more, you need to understand and address two basic problems. The first is knowing how to discuss money with your boss. The second and far more important challenge is knowing how to align your self-interest with your boss's. Put yourself in your boss's shoes: What absolutely needs to get done and how can you help accomplish those goals? Once you're thinking performance first, pay second, you can begin to ask using one of my favorite acronyms: **MORE.**

M → MEET FACE-TO-FACE: THE OPENING CONVERSATION TO GET MORE

The real way to ask for a raise isn't to start with the money talk. Rather, the goal is to initiate a dialogue with your boss. This brings us to the "M" in **MORE**—meeting face-to-face. You want in-person discussions about the boss's priorities and short-term goals and how you can contribute to team success in a big way. Taking on more and larger responsibilities is a natural pivot to discuss how you're compensated.

Before you meet with your boss, think about leverage—and who has it. For example, are you easily replaceable? Do you have skills that nobody else has? What's your endgame—the next step on your career path?

"Scott" was obsessed with making more money. I knew him socially, back in the day, and he talked more about the size of his salary than anything else. You know the type: the sports car, the nice watch, the suit. Any time he wanted a new toy, he'd brag that all he had to do was pretend he had another offer and tell his boss he was going to leave.

One day, Scott really did have an offer—a double-your-salary opportunity. He expected to waltz into his boss's office, flash that letter, and get his salary doubled. Instead, his boss told him, "Sounds like a great opportunity. Good luck to you."

Weeks later, I ran into Scott and asked how his new job was going. He said something about it not working out. "I got in over my head."

I began to get the picture. Scott might have been able to convince his old boss for a while that he was a real rainmaker, but the new company saw right through him: no substance.

Then, in Scott's only moment of humility I ever witnessed, he admitted to having begged his former boss to get his old job back. "I had to take a cut," he mumbled. "Like 20 percent from what I was making before."

The leverage, as it turned out, was in his boss's corner.

Asking for and ultimately receiving more money requires a PLAN. The more you PLAN, the better you can shape the money conversation to be more about performance than just about pay. Otherwise, figure out how you're going to ask and hope for the best.

PLAN

Positivity: You must approach this conversation positively, not negatively. There are people who give energy and those who suck energy. Your boss will be far more receptive if you're sunny rather than a downer—he or she doesn't need another problem.

Loyalty: You want to convey a sense of loyalty to the job, to the boss, to the company. You're all in, not only for what needs to be done but also for how you do it.

Accomplishments: You need accomplishments, not just activity. Players aren't rewarded for simply shooting—the ball has to go through the net, that's how the team wins. It's the same in business. Make a list of what you're actually accomplishing to help your team win.

No: What if that's the answer? What will your reaction be? Before you start the conversation, you need to have a Plan B, just in case things don't go exactly as you hope. First, stay positive. Second, try doing more. Third, start targeting opportunities both inside the company and elsewhere—what other companies, industries, and roles interest you? Then you can begin to network with people who can help you get where you want to go.

YOU AND YOUR BOSS: SELF-INTERESTS ALIGNED

Guess what? Your boss wants to make more money, too. That means you and your boss are actually aligned in your respective self-interests. So by focusing on achieving short-term goals and deliverables, you and your boss both can get what you want. That's an entirely different conversation than just you asking for money!

You need to engage with your boss in ongoing discussions about how *you both* can do better and how *you* can make a bigger impact on team success.

The dialogue needs to be focused on what you are contributing now and what you can do to expand your responsibilities and scope. Ask your boss, "What does our team need that isn't being done now? How can I contribute?" This isn't kissing up. You're acting like a partner who is focused on deliverables.

You haven't abandoned your self-interest; you just linked it to achieving your boss's short-term goals. Believe me, your boss will welcome more partnership and greater alignment around priorities and objectives. This is a conversation your boss wants to have with you, instead of listening to endless complaints about money.

PREPARE, PREPARE, PREPARE

The most obvious advice for asking for a raise is often the most forgotten:
• Write down your best case in terms your bosses will understand quickly.
• Focus on what matters most to your boss and the team.

Trust me, managers are more impressed when employees can clearly show how they saved the company money, boosted sales, or exceeded other quantitative metrics. Don't leave off qualitative accomplishments, either. Bosses often appreciate employees who decreased their own stress levels or showed leadership under pressure.

Offense vs. Defense

OFFENSE: Focus on achieving your boss's short-term goals and objectives. Make an immediate impact. You and your boss are on the same team and, together, moving toward the goal line.

DEFENSE: Complain constantly about your pay to any and all who will listen. Avoid doing anything beyond the absolute minimum. Now you and your boss are opposing each other.

Which position would you rather play to win?

KNOW
THY BOSS

You won't be able to make a partner out of any boss, though, if you don't know with whom you are dealing. Just as poorly as people ask for raises, bosses can fumble the requests as well. Some get flustered. Some delay. And some are, well, just bad bosses.

Here are a few of the types you might come across in your career. Knowing in advance if you're facing one of these should vary your MORE strategy and shift your PLAN.

STONE-FACED SALLY has the uncanny ability to shut down virtually every facial muscle the moment the word "money" comes up. These bosses have learned over the years that the more silent they are, the more people who want a raise will stumble on their words, looking so weak they'll rarely ask again. If you're facing Sally, stay steady. Be a little silent yourself during the conversation and take a Zen-like approach that throws off her guard.

BEST-FRIEND BILL can put on a performance worthy of a Broadway star. Unable to come up with any better excuse, these bosses pretend they'll "do their best" to help you get a raise and "take it to the very top" if need be. You can tell the sincere boss from the phony when you get the arm-around-the-shoulder treatment and concerned looks that couldn't be more fake. When facing Best-Friend Bill, hold his feet to the fire and propose follow-up meetings.

In subtle and nonthreatening ways, let this boss know you are on to the game-playing.

FAKE-NEWS FRANNY is the kind of boss who'll make up stories, such as suggesting you're already "way up in salary" when you know (having done your research!) that this boss is flat-out lying. This person isn't too much different from ...

POOR-MOUTH MATT will swear by all he holds dear that he's facing many of the same financial struggles you are. No matter how much these bosses say they sympathize, though, they just won't help. Sadly, the truth may be that their own compensation won't be quite as fat if too many raises are handed out. Whatever the reason, the roar of Poor-Mouth Matt's cherry-red Porsche pulling into the office parking lot each morning is a dead giveaway he's hardly in your shoes.

O → OWN YOUR OBJECTIVES: DO MORE TO EARN MORE

No one is going to promote you or give you more money just because you decide so. Time in a chair does not automatically entitle you to a prize, as if your career is some kind of endurance contest. This brings us to the "O" in getting **MORE**—you need to own your performance objectives. Set expectations with your boss for what you're going to deliver and when. Establish a series of check-ins with your boss to make sure you're on track and to update him or her on what's been accomplished. This will not only ensure that your efforts are focused on what's most meaningful to the boss and the team's performance, but you'll also increase your chances of becoming an outlier on performance. That's how you get to be an outlier on pay, too—by being indispensable and as close as it gets to being irreplaceable.

ESTABLISH A SERIES OF CHECK-INS WITH YOUR BOSS.

While I was visiting one of Korn Ferry's European offices not that long ago, I was approached by an employee. Over my many weeks of traveling all over the continent, meeting with hundreds of people, this conversation really stayed with me. I was struck by how this employee spoke up and framed her request for advice. She told me she enjoys working for our firm and is very satisfied with her job but was unsure of how to expand her role. She wanted to know how to best approach her boss for more responsibilities.

I could tell that she also wanted more money, but to her credit, she never said that outright. Instead, she emphasized her desire to make a bigger impact in the firm. I offered her some impromptu coaching on how to ask her boss for more and bigger assignments. "Learn more, do more," I told her, "and the money will follow."

MORE
THAN JUST
MONEY

When you think about compensation, the first thing that comes to mind is, of course, money! But there are other forms of compensation, such as additional paid time off, flexible work hours, or (depending on your level in the organization) stock options. Your boss may not be able to grant you a fat raise, but getting another week or two of paid vacation can work out nearly the same, math-wise.

If your role is changing, you may be able to negotiate perks that will help your performance and supplement your base salary. Say you're taking on a sales position involving heavy travel and you don't own a car. Your company may be willing to make the lease payments—that can be negotiated. Or maybe your new role requires lots of late nights entertaining clients; you can negotiate higher travel expenses and raise your per diem limits.

Other perks that can be negotiated, but that employees seldom think about, include flexible work hours, virtual working arrangements, additional vacation time, tuition or professional development reimbursement, gym memberships and other wellness programs, additional insurance, and commuting costs, among others.

When you're taking a new job, there are other financial benefits that can be negotiated once you have a written offer in hand: signing bonuses, higher commission rates, bonuses, and stock-option grants. Since you're going to start an ongoing conversation with your new boss (you are, right?), you can also set up a plan for early reviews for raises. Depending on your organization and position level, equity and profit-sharing agreements can also be put on the table as options.

Also, negotiate your way out as you're on your way in. Don't be blinded by thoughts of happily ever after. What happens if it doesn't work out? Think about severance, noncompete clauses, and so forth.

R → RESEARCH THE MARKET: DO YOUR HOMEWORK TO GET MORE

Don't just assume you're underpaid. The "R" in getting **MORE** is doing your research. No matter what you might think about your paycheck, you can't just pick numbers randomly or decide you really need to make X to support your lifestyle. It isn't that your boss doesn't care that you have expenses for your children's education or that you want to take the entire family on vacation. But that's not how raises work!

It's like selling your house: you need comps. Go to Zillow.com and you can instantly see what other houses in your neighborhood are going for. In the same way, Korn Ferry Advance can provide salary comparisons. Job sites can give you an idea of what different positions pay. Start networking: ask recruiters and reach out to friends. Maybe your company is doing poorly, or your industry is depressed. Without that market intelligence, you don't know how you're priced—above market, below market, or fair value.

Whatever you do, don't start the watercooler cesspool by asking everyone how much they're making. This could possibly end in your jealousy or envy but will probably end ultimately with negative team karma. You don't have to be wallpaper, just be discreet.

All this homework goes a long way in giving you a little edge in every conversation about money. For example, my own company puts out annual global predictions for raises in the coming year that can be incredibly handy when numbers are discussed. Along with citing each profession, it gives some perspective on topics like cost of living and inflation. Finally, be realistic. If you're asking for a 50 percent raise, you need to think this through very carefully. If it's 10 percent, that's a whole different story. Although it isn't necessarily your problem, you should consider fairness. If you're given a 20 percent raise, what about your colleagues? You won't naturally think this way, but your boss should. This awareness is all about putting yourself in your boss's shoes: *what's in it for me* versus *what's in it for you.*

A CAREER PATH—
NOT A CAREEN PATH

Be warned—if you earn more, more is going to be expected of you. While that seems obvious, too many people miss this point when asking for a raise. They focus on the bling of a higher salary without considering the expectations that go along with it. I'm constantly amazed by people who look at a job or a particular role and say, "That looks easy, I could do that." (If that were the case, we'd all be the starting quarterback for the New York Jets.) Be honest with yourself: Can you really do the job? If your cell phone rings on Saturday morning and it's your boss or your biggest client, are you ready to pick up? Or are you the type to let it go to voicemail and deal with it on Monday, because the weekend is *your time*?

Know what you're getting into. That bigger number on your paycheck will always come with a price. It's up to you to decide what's reasonable and acceptable for your life. If you make the wrong move, your career path will become a "careen path," and you'll find yourself running straight into a brick wall.

"Jeff" is a contractor with his own small business. When I saw him recently, Jeff told me about a friend of his who works in financial services. "He's making $200,000 a year and he's done by 3 p.m.," Jeff said. "Why am I working so hard for a lot less than that? He says he can get me an interview. What do you think?"

"Don't you dare even think about it!" I told him. "It's not who you are. You're a 'let's go fishing' guy who would rather wear jeans than go to a networking party in a suit."

Jeff was taken aback. Clearly, he was thinking seriously about making this change.

"Your friend isn't buying and selling stocks," I explained, "he's asking people to become clients so the firm can manage their money. To be successful at that, you'd have to be a schmoozer—go to parties, meet people. You need a big network of people. Does that sound like you?"

Jeff shook his head.

"I know it's tempting when you think about the money, but it would soon turn into a nightmare. And trust me, your friend didn't start out making $200,000," I said.

For Jeff, it was about changing careers, but the same thing can happen to anyone who pursues a much bigger job without thinking seriously about how prepared they are for that step or how well this job would suit them. Have you really learned and grown sufficiently to take on the added responsibilities of this new position? The last thing you want to do is get promoted into a job in which you're over your head (the Peter Principle in action) or find yourself in a job that demands long hours and expectations of extra effort that you can't meet.

E → ENVISION YOUR ENDGAME: HOW TO GET MORE OF WHAT MATTERS

Money is the by-product of a well-managed career path. That's where the "E" of getting **MORE** comes in—envisioning your endgame. To take control of your career development, you need to define your end goal and what it looks like to you—a better job, more challenges, and new opportunities to grow. As you do more, you will probably get MORE.

1 **Do your homework.** Don't just assume you are underpaid because you want or need more money.

2 **Your boss just isn't that into your salary.** You may spend most of your time thinking about how much (or little) you're paid, but your boss doesn't. Your boss is focused on team performance (and his or her own paycheck).

3 **Initiate an ongoing dialogue with your boss.** Performance isn't a once-a-year task, so don't depend on a one-time summit meeting with your boss at performance-review time. You need to have an ongoing conversation about deliverables.

4 **Be an outlier on performance.** If you want a larger-than-average pay raise you need to do more—not just meeting but exceeding expectations.

5 **Don't make the wrong move.** It's a classic case of "the grass is always greener" syndrome. You think a new job will be so much better than the one you have, especially if it pays more money. Look before you make the leap; otherwise, you could make a wrong move that derails your career.

6 **Beware the competing job offer.** It's a strategy that works—sometimes. Research shows that getting an offer from another company (and be prepared to show evidence that this is real, not just a threat on your part) can make you more valuable in your current employer's eyes. And if you're seen as a valuable contributor, it's cheaper for your company to give you an extra 10 percent or so than recruit, hire, and onboard a replacement. Just beware of the risks. If the company can't afford you or if you aren't "worth" the extra money, your boss may shake your hand and wish you well. Be prepared to go if it comes to that.

MORE IS ALL ABOUT TAKING CONTROL

One final note: MORE is not something you get. It's about the value you bring and being rewarded for it. Take control (a theme of this book, as should be pretty obvious by now). Learn more, stretch yourself, and in time you will earn more. And your rewards will be more than money.

YOUR 5 TAKEAWAYS

FOR ASKING FOR MORE MONEY

Asking your boss for a raise shouldn't be a "one and done" exchange. It's an ongoing conversation about short-term goals and deliverables and your accomplishments.

Don't just make up a number—do your research. Understand the market for your position, industry, and geographic region.

Define the quantifiable benefits you bring. What have you done that improves the team's performance and advances the boss's objectives?

Remember: learn more, earn more. Be aligned with your boss about how you can stretch and grow in taking on more of what needs to be done.

Keep the end goal in mind. You won't be in this current job that long. Learn all you can now so you can position yourself for bigger responsibilities and higher pay next time.

Part Two

...BUT IT'S NOT ABOUT YOU

Unless you're a sculptor working alone in your studio, chipping marble or molding clay, you are not a solo performer. Despite all the technological advancements of the past few decades, we still need to work with others.

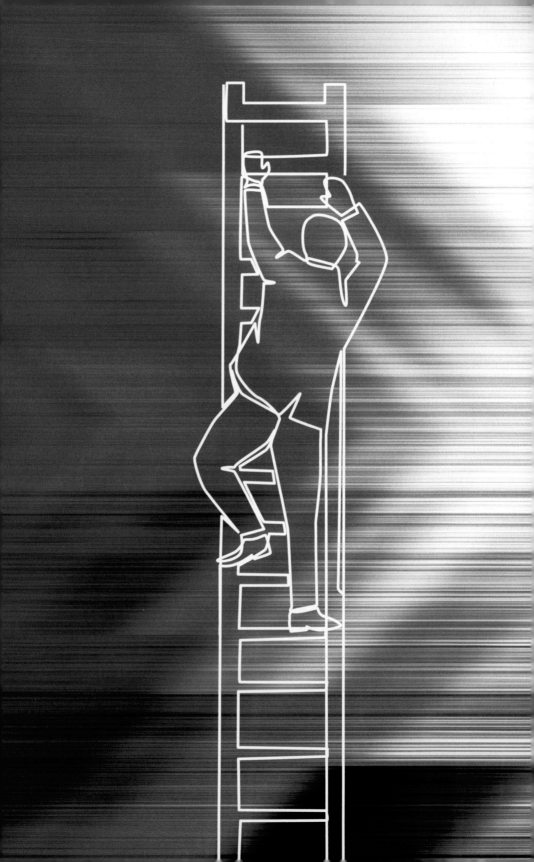

Chapter Four

SURVIVING BAD BOSSES:

It's Not Them, It's You

Good bosses are amazing role models who embody the behaviors they want to see in others. And there's nothing like working for a great boss who champions and mentors you, invests in your success and development, and gives you ample opportunities to learn and grow. But that's *not* what we're talking about here. Good happens about a third to half of the time, and great is a rare bird indeed.

BAD BOSSES COME IN ALL STRIPES AND TYPES AND CAN UNDERCUT AND CRUSH AMBITION.

Far more common, unfortunately, is having a bad boss. Some bosses are only mildly bad, but be prepared to endure some really treacherous ones in the course of your career.

The way a truly bad boss behaves can just make you cringe. They're hypercritical, unsupportive, sarcastic, negative, insecure, self-centered, unapproachable, unreliable, and outright duplicitous. Bad bosses come in all stripes and types and can undercut and crush ambition in ways both subtle and obvious.

As a CEO, I'm sometimes asked why companies can't reign in the bad-boss phenomenon. Believe me, corporate America has come a long way toward trying to curtail hostile work environments—it's the law, after all. But there is so much other behavior that is impossible to regulate and that HR departments struggle to stay on top of. There's the boss who always praises you to your face, yet the lack of promotions or raises tells you the boss disdains your efforts—and maybe you, personally. Then there's the boss who's always in a rotten mood. You can hear it in the terse com-

Q I hate my boss! My boss is manipulative, plays favorites, and doesn't give me the credit I deserve. Some days I just want to walk out the door. What can I do?

A Don't quit! If you can't bear it, then you need an exit strategy. If you decide to stay, you need to make it workable for yourself by managing your relationship with your bad boss, starting with better communication. It could help turn things around. The good news is you never stay with one boss very long. Soon, you or the boss will move on.

ments and see it in the eye-rolling and headshaking. And you can feel how much that boss wants you to leave his or her office, stop talking at a meeting, or in the worst cases, be fired.

THE BOOK ON BAD BOSS BEHAVIOR

The problem with bad bosses is so pervasive, there's an astounding amount of research devoted to this topic. There are bosses who:

✔ Put up one obstacle after another to block their employees' growth and development.

✔ Want people to do well, but not so well that they're considered as good as the boss, or maybe even better.

✔ Favor one or a few people who, although seemingly incompetent and lazy, keep getting the best assignments and the most public praises.

✔ Refuse to give the hardest-working employees a word of feedback or, heaven forbid, a compliment.

✔ Talk trash about others behind their backs.

✔ Refuse to delegate responsibility or authority.

✔ Have a "meeting after the meeting," purposefully leaving key people out of them.

Typically, I hear bad-boss stories from people who've quit their jobs. The sad truth is people don't leave companies, they leave bosses. So, let's start right there. Resist the temptation to quit. However, yes, anything out of bounds or that violates harassment policies and laws is a different story. Then you need to file a complaint with human resources.

If you have a difficult boss and you just can't see yourself working for him or her much longer, then you need an exit strategy. If you're actively networking inside and outside your company (see Chapter Eleven, "Networking Within"), then you're already investigating opportunities, internally and externally. Until you depart to that great new job, you need to make the best of a difficult situation.

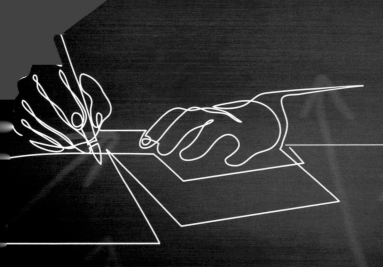

Your Bad-Boss Management Game Plan

UNDERSTAND. Consider the boss's motivations, goals, and priorities.

COMMUNICATE. Relationships often fail simply due to a lack of communication. Your relationship with the boss is no different.

PERFORM. Always orient back to very short-term objectives and goals.

BUILD TRUST. When there is trust in what you've done, there will likely be belief in what you say.

PERSONAL? BUSINESS? IT'S BOTH!

You can survive a bad boss—it's a skill you can actually learn. Even when you work for a bad or bumbling boss, you can find a way to rise above. Sure, in any other context, you'd avoid these people like the plague. But you're stuck with them for now (short job tenure can really be your friend), eight-plus hours a day. Know this: with all due respect to *The Godfather*, Michael Corleone was wrong when he declared, "It's not personal, it's strictly business." When it comes to dealing with bad bosses, it's both.

Here's a classic bad-boss story I heard the other day. Everything sounded so great for this manager when he interviewed at a small but fast-growing company. The boss was outgoing and personable and had promised, "There's a long runway for you here."

Then, on the very first day, things went south—and fast.

First, there was no "parking space with your name on it" as the manager had been promised (nor was there a car allowance—promised, but not in writing). The admin who was supposed to be dedicated to him was actually shared by a team of 12. The "office with a view" turned out to be small, windowless, and shared with someone else two days a week. The real kicker, though, was his first meeting with his boss to go over the department budget.

When the manager zeroed in on the year-to-year comparisons for salaries, he couldn't believe what he was seeing: he was making significantly less than his predecessor—the exact opposite of what his boss had told him. The manager could hear the echo of their salary negotiations, when the boss had assured him, "I'm doing the best I can for you, but things are tight around here, and we may need to let a few people go. You're making a lot more than the person you replaced."

The boss reached over and, almost with a sleight of hand, gathered up the budget printouts. "Can you believe they gave me the wrong ones?" Flashing a smile, the boss left and came back 10 minutes later with a new printout.

The year-ago figures were gone—and so was the manager's optimism for this new job. All he could ask himself was, "If this is day one, what's the rest of my time going to be like with this guy?"

When you're dealing with a bad boss, you need a game plan—not just the same plan of trying to "do your job" and ignore the boss. That's impossible. It's time to take control.

UNDERSTANDING THE BOSS

What makes your boss tick in a very broad way? What is his or her MO or behavior patterns? In addition to that, what do you know about them personally? Review the boss's LinkedIn page or read what he or she posts on social media for deeper insights.

As you understand these basics of the boss's behavior, you can start to employ some basic strategies for dealing with some of the common types of difficult bosses.

THE MANIPULATOR

These characters are known for being cunning to get whatever they need, and they're experts at playing people to their advantage. One way to deal with Manipulators is to hold them accountable. That'll take a little more effort on your part, but it's preferable to spinning your wheels in 10 different directions.

Let's say you work for a Manipulator who asks you to undertake a specific task or assignment. A week later, though, he or she claims that a completely different request was made. What can you do? Consider this game plan:

- ✔ **VOLUNTEER** at the next team meeting to take notes and document the discussion.

- ✔ **FOLLOW UP** with a brief memo and email to the boss and team, listing who was assigned what and the due date.

- ✔ **MAINTAIN** good communication with the boss and the others on the team.

When what was agreed to is spelled out, the Manipulator can't start sending people in circles. The Manipulator won't change overnight, but at least you'll reduce or even eliminate one common source of frustration: Why did you say you wanted me to do *A* if you really wanted me to do *B*?

THE MICROMANAGER

While not exactly a bad boss, the Micromanager can be annoying to say the least. Also, micromanaging is one of the most common complaints about bosses. Identifying characteristics of the Micromanager include heavy scrutiny, constant texting and emailing to "check on things," and passive-aggressive comments. Micromanaging may be hardwired into the boss's personality. Here are some tips for managing the Micromanager and building trust over time:

FIGURE OUT THE CAUSE. Odds are, the boss's micromanagement is all about his or her need to keep control because of fear, insecurity, or anxiety. For example, it can be really hard for a middle manager, especially someone new to the role, to be responsible for reporting the results of the team while not being able to control the behaviors and results of individuals or the entire team. (Later, when you become the manager, take heed that you don't fall into this trap. Remember: you're learning what *not* to do when you're the boss.) Your strategy is to find out what's causing your boss so much anxiety. Does the boss have quotas to meet? Does he or she have a new boss who is very demanding? You may not be able to start out by asking these questions directly, but you can find out more about the boss's main goals for the year and how you can help. (You should be doing this anyway—remember the discussion on getting more money in Chapter Three, "Making More Money.") If you ask the questions and truly listen for the answers, then you've positioned yourself as being part of the solution, not adding to the problem.

APPLY REVERSE MICRO-MANAGEMENT. If information is what makes your boss feel better (i.e., more in control), then give the boss more information before he or she asks for it. This is a little "reverse micromanagement" that makes you more proactive than reactive. It can be as simple as sending an email with your plan for the day or week before your boss asks what you're working on. You can take it to the next step by sending an email at the end of the day or week to summarize what you've accomplished and what will come next. Over time, this flow of information builds trust, and your boss may loosen the reins a little bit.

PICK YOUR BATTLES. Micromanagers are typically world-champion nitpickers. Not every issue is worth addressing, and you'll probably have to let some things go. Save your energy and attention for what really matters. Otherwise, you run the risk of having the boss think you're challenging his or her authority or that you're being a nitpicker yourself. If you choose your battles, you may become less emotional, which could make your boss more likely to listen and engage with you.

GAIN SOME CONTROL— GRADUALLY. Trust can be built slowly over time. Sometimes it's a gain of only inches, and it must be done artfully. As you establish rapport with your boss by doing the steps outlined thus far (such as being proactive with information and picking your battles on what to take issue with), you can bring up the issue of trust. For example, ask your boss:

"I notice that you spend a lot of time checking my work. Is there anything I can do to improve so you'll trust me more?" That opens the dialogue for setting expectations and the boss's need for feedback from you.

SET BOUNDARIES. Your micromanager may want to see or hear from you 24-7, but that could be a recipe for frustration and burnout. A smarter approach is to be available, but not every minute of the day. Identify those times that are sacred to you and prioritize them. Unless there is an urgent issue or an emergency, it's OK to contact your boss after you've had dinner with your family or in the morning after you awaken, instead of reaching for your phone at the bedside in the middle of the night to return a text. Your pattern of responding will set expectations for your boss, too. When your boss understands that you don't typically respond after certain hours, then those nonurgent texts will probably become less frequent and the after-hours emails will be prefaced with, "When you have time tomorrow, could you …"

YOU CAN'T CHANGE YOUR BOSS (BUT YOU WILL CHANGE BOSSES)

Studying and categorizing—these are critical steps to take on the road to bad-boss management. But one of the biggest mistakes people make with bosses is focusing on trying to change them. That won't work. It's all about *you* adjusting, shifting—not trying to change the boss.

It's time to turn feelings and emotions (the intangible) into actions (the tangible). When things become a little less subjective, you can become more objective.

Since *you* are the only one you can change, you need to address your own attitudes and behaviors. You need to dissect the problem, not to assign blame or seek vindication for how unfairly you're being treated. Pinpoint the problem and its cause, so you can find a solution. And here's the good news: no matter what the problem turns out to be, you hold that solution. By becoming more self-aware of your attitudes, judgments, behaviors, and tendency to react negatively, you can defuse a lot of the tension. Keep in mind a saying you may have heard from couple's or family counseling: when one person changes, everybody starts to shift.

> PINPOINT THE PROBLEM AND ITS CAUSE, SO YOU CAN FIND A SOLUTION.

This is an opportunity to learn and grow as you control your emotions, manage your behaviors, and determine how best to respond—and when not to. The result will be less stress for you and a more manageable working relationship with your boss.

There is another consolation. Bad bosses teach you how not to be.

It's true—people are much more likely to learn about compassion and integrity from a bad boss than a good one. (Of course, there are those situations in which people perpetuate bad behaviors learned from others.)

When you know firsthand how horrible it feels to be subjected to a bad boss's behavior, it's highly unlikely that you'd ever do that to someone else. So while there's some short-term pain, the long-term gain is greater self-awareness and a deeper realization of the importance of valuing others.

Then, in time, you'll move on, smarter and more experienced for having worked for this bad boss who taught you lessons about coping with difficulties and facing challenges head-on.

COMMUNICATE:
KEEPING THE LINES OPEN

Without communication, no relationship can last. So if your boss shuts you out—or you respond by trying to freeze out your boss—you've lost already. Whatever the problem you're having with your boss, you need to find a way to discuss the situation. Most important, it must be *nonconfrontational*.

You aren't accusing your boss or anyone of anything. You just want to express your concerns and find a way to re-establish the relationship. Ask for a face-to-face meeting with your boss. Explain that you've noticed a change in your interactions with him or her and ask what you can do differently. By your words, and soon by your actions, you're demonstrating that you're committed to changing.

Communicating with your boss also requires you to become more attuned to others' behaviors and cues (verbal and nonverbal). Take a good look at yourself, too. Even if you are a cut above the rest, you are responsible for your own behavior and for reducing negativity—and that includes what you say and how you say it.

Your main objective in communicating with your boss is to find out how you can help change things. You want to be more effective and helpful to the team. If you don't know what to say, then start there: "What can I do to be more effective?"

The Shutout

What happens when a good relationship with your boss turns sour? You can feel blindsided and unsure of what happened. You may fear losing your job. Let's say things have been going along pretty well with your boss. Then suddenly, things change. The boss is going to other people on the team. A project that should have been yours went to someone else. At the last team meeting, every one of your suggestions was shot down, while every word your colleagues uttered earned the boss's praise as the most brilliant ideas ever (or so you perceive).

If you're being shut out, you need to take control and communicate with your boss. You may find that your boss has experienced a change in your behavior. Perhaps you seem disengaged or increasingly dismissive. Now that you've made it easier for the boss to give you feedback, you can clear things up.

PERFORM: KEEP A SHORT-TERM FOCUS

The bulk of your communication with your boss is likely to be around what needs to be done and how you can help make that happen. So you need to make sure you're performing. When you're unhappy with someone, it's too easy to turn passive-aggressive. The boss wants something done today; you decide you'll get around to it—eventually. This will only perpetuate unhealthy conflict and, ultimately, become self-destructive.

Stay focused on what needs to be done, especially in the very short term. What project or task has the highest priority? What needs to be done right now? Staying engaged with the work will help you rise above your negative feelings, and you'll communicate more frequently and purposefully with your boss. Ironically, this is essentially the same advice for getting more money (see Chapter Three, "Making More Money"). It's all about knowing the boss's goals and priorities and making them your priorities too.

WHAT IF IT'S YOU?

It's also possible that at least part of your conflict with your boss is rooted in your own misperceptions about this relationship and how you think the boss should treat you. Here are eye-opening possibilities to consider:

→ **The boss doesn't think you're as good as you think you are.**
→ **You're jealous the boss got the job you thought you should have.**
→ **You don't respect your boss's abilities.**
→ **You and your boss are a mismatch in terms of style, motivation, and how work gets done.**
→ **Your personalities clash.**

If you know what's at the heart of this problem, you can do your part to fix it: understand, communicate, perform, and build trust.

BUILD TRUST

As much you might want to push back right now—*it's not me, it's the boss!*—remember, objectivity is your friend. The fact is, we trust people for two basic reasons. One, we have confidence in their competence. Two, we believe that they have our best intentions at heart. We're drawn to those we perceive as competent and reliable. We want to have a relationship with them. But if we feel there's a reason to be guarded around them, we shut them out.

Trust can erode if people begin to doubt you or your motivations. Maybe you're perceived as a threat to your manager's authority or position. Maybe it seemed you took a little too much credit for that last big team win. Maybe the boss's boss is paying a little too much attention to you, and your boss feels that you're playing politics.

You won't know if you don't ask. Once again, communication is the lifeline for any relationship. But talk is cheap, as they say, if you don't perform—and that's what will establish or build trust. When there is trust in what you've done, there will likely be belief in what you say.

Let's say you've had a great relationship with your boss, but suddenly the boss seems a little evasive. In initiating a conversation to find out if there is something you can do, you may hear an entirely different story. It may be that the boss is preoccupied with an overwhelming deadline. Now your question of "how can I be more effective?" may be the start of your taking on more responsibilities or stretching yourself into a new role because the boss needs your help.

You Aren't the Center of the Boss's Universe

Regardless of what you've done (or not done), your boss has a lot more to think about than just you. There are just too many people, projects, and priorities that need to be managed. Compartmentalization is a must-have skill for bosses, and those who are the most senior and seasoned will probably never show what's going on in their personal life— no matter how upsetting or even tragic. But some bosses, particularly newer managers, probably have not yet mastered the art of compartmentalizing. As a result, if the boss is busy with his or her own projects, or feeling frustrated about something else, you could be encountering that moody trickle-down effect.

YOUR 5 TAKEAWAYS

FOR MANAGING YOUR BAD BOSS

You can't change your boss—you can only change yourself. Or you can change the situation by developing an exit strategy.

Understanding your boss's behaviors and motivations will help you move away from blame and feeling victimized, and learn how to manage the relationship.

Communicate, communicate, communicate. If you don't do the communicating, then somebody else will—and it will probably be about you.

Be accountable for your own behaviors and performance, and always ask for unvarnished feedback.

Trust is built by you—saying what you mean and doing what you say.

Chapter Five

COPING WITH COWORKERS:

The Good, the Bad, and the Utterly Annoying

We move now from the person in charge of your job to another workplace relationship: the one you have with your colleagues. Think about it. We sit around these people. We talk to them on the phone. We go to lunch with some of them. And then we go home and usually blab about them to anybody who will listen. Sometimes we treat them like strangers, not even giving them the courtesy of a simple hello. But, strangers or not, you can't afford to ignore colleagues. They have a bigger impact on your career, let alone your happiness, than just about anybody else in your life.

Their power is enormous. We've all written that email we wish we could get back, and it's your colleagues who can decide whether or not to hit the dreaded forward button. Or perhaps you've inadvertently shown your anger during a meeting—it's your colleagues who decide whether to gossip about that episode within earshot of your boss (which naturally happens just when you've asked for a raise). They can decide to treat your presentation like a work of genius or pull the silent treatment during every word you say.

Simply through their own behavior toward you, or through side comments about you, it's your colleagues who can be the grand arbiters of whether you are considered a good culture fit or a malcontent. And no matter how many jobs you hop around to, your reputation transcends.

The point is, you need to respect your coworkers in all the ways that word means—as individuals who are important, as workers who are valuable to the company, and as the very people who *can make or break you.*

Everyone Matters

Assistants, the mailroom clerk, the receptionist—the best companies long ago realized their value. Never make the mistake of treating "low-level" folks dismissively. Do that and you're not only breaking the Golden Rule of how to treat others, you're also taking the risk that these people might complain about you. Even if they don't, colleagues who notice your rudeness—*and some will*—are going to remember. It will come out during one of those 360-degree performance reviews or get leaked to your superiors in other ways.

Your manager's assistant is particularly critical. I've seen people's entire careers falter because they've underestimated the access the assistant has. Who do you think is letting your boss know that you take forever to respond to emails or frequently blow off procedural budget questions? Think of how much time you spend talking to your boss one-on-one. Now multiply that tenfold for the assistant whose pen you just "borrowed" off his or her desk and never returned.

Q Help! My coworkers are so annoying. How can I possibly work with these people?

A As long as people live and work in groups, there's going to be conflict. Everybody is different. Be discerning: Are you annoyed by this person's personality traits? (If so, then you're going to have to deal with it.) Or is it because of his or her behaviors? (In which case you need to figure out if you should say something and how.) Your emotional intelligence, interpersonal savvy, and communication skills are at work!

COWORKERS WHO MAKE YOU CRAZY

Over the years, you'll have coworkers who feel like family. And there will be some you could probably do without.

Face it, no matter where you work, you'll find people who annoy you. Some are difficult, some are negative, and some butt heads with you over every plan and project—just for the sport of it. I'm sure you've seen some of these behaviors. There are people who:

- ✔ Think everything is about them (therefore they should get everything)
- ✔ Think they're smarter than everyone else
- ✔ Try to make themselves look "so busy" but spend most of their time avoiding work and pushing it off on others
- ✔ Take all the credit for successes—and throw others under the bus for failures
- ✔ Undermine you at every turn, especially with the boss

- ✔ Say "yes, yes, yes" to what needs to be done, but afterward it's all "no, no, no"
- ✔ Gossip about everyone and everything
- ✔ Are excuse machines when it comes to explaining why their work is late or why they aren't available to work after hours
- ✔ Put off starting the project until the last minute and then beg everyone to help
- ✔ *And so much more …*

It's different, of course, but there are many parallels between dealing with annoying colleagues and dealing with bad bosses. In both cases, you need to figure out what's manageable and what's unbearable. As you progress along the scale from "a little annoyed" to "tearing out your hair," you need to ramp up your exit strategy. In between, there are coping strategies to help you manage your coworker situation. But first you need to discern the problem.

THE CHRONIC COMPLAINERS

WHISPERS AT THE WATERCOOLER SPREAD NEGATIVITY LIKE THE PLAGUE.

Airplanes, restaurants, the workplace. These three are the worst places on the planet for spawning complainers. In the air, it comes from being strapped in among strangers at 35,000 feet—plus delays, lost luggage, and the toenail-clipper sitting next to you. In restaurants, being served by someone brings out the complainer in most people: *The soup's too hot ... The soup's too cold ... Are you sure it's vegan? It tastes like veggie.* When I was in high school, I lasted one six-hour shift working in a restaurant—I just couldn't take it.

The real cesspool of constant complaining, though, is the workplace, where whispers at the watercooler spread negativity like the plague. I learned this many years ago when I was working at a consulting firm. Seven of us were on a project together. We had different backgrounds and perspectives, which should have made us highly innovative. Except one of our teammates was "Debby Downer." With every scenario, Debby *only* saw the worst possible outcome. She shot down new ideas like a skeet shooter at target practice. *That will never work … We tried that before … It's just too risky … No one will go for it … How's that going to work with the budget we have?*

Debby wasn't intentionally trying to derail the team; she was just hardwired never to see the blue sky—only "the sky is falling." The problem was that with Debby around, even great ideas turned into bad ideas. She brought us all down—really down. In the end, the constant complaining was so emotionally taxing on the team, we were not successful.

If you're a chronic complainer, you're draining energy.

I'm not complaining! I actually welcome complaints that bring issues out into the open—with one important caveat: complaining needs to be "constructive"—that is, accompanied by an idea, a solution, or at least some additional insight. Otherwise, it's just whining. Constructive complaining actually generates energy that can be channeled into finding solutions.

Here's how "constructive complaining" can help you:

YOU CAN'T COMPLAIN ABOUT WHAT YOU CREATE. Sometimes I feel like the chief complaint officer. It comes with the job, because by the time issues get escalated to me, it's really a problem. When fielding complaints, my number one rule for myself and others is never to complain about a decision or a situation you created. Own it! It's the fastest way to change your karma from being the victim of circumstances to being empowered to change them. Take control and find an option—Door A, B, or C. You'll start moving in a different direction and take yourself from "helpless and hopeless" to "helpful and happier."

BE IN THE SOLUTIONS BUSINESS. It's so easy to be in the problems business—there's always a situation or circumstance to complain about. But you want to be in the solutions business. I received this advice soon after I became CEO. At one of my first board meetings, I raised problem after problem. Someone pulled me aside afterward and told me, "If you want advice, fine. But come to the board with ideas of what to do. You need to be the solutions person, not the complaint guy." The same goes for you, too: be the one who suggests a solution. Even if it's ultimately not the right answer, it will help create positive momentum.

CREATE A CULTURE OF CONSTRUCTIVE COMPLAINING. There's nothing inherently wrong with complaints, the same way there's nothing wrong with conflict. Both can actually spark the creative process as people own the problem and brainstorm with each other. Over time, constructive complaining (along with creative conflict) can forge a culture in which people aren't afraid to speak the truth, take on issues, and find new ways forward.

BANISH THE "BUT." Nothing shoots down a group discussion faster than "but." One person floats an idea, and another jumps in with "but" (or similar negative words and nonverbals). *That's an interesting idea but the problem is ...* What comes next is always negative, and it invariably leads to disagreement. To improve team effectiveness, I suggest replacing "but" with "and." *That's an interesting idea, and you might also consider X.* You can actually feel the energy in the room start to rise.

You Never Know
Who's Behind That Door

Another problem with gripe-fests in the workplace is that they tend to happen in some secret "safe" place, like the bathroom. It's as if it's the confessional, complete with angels on the ceiling. People think it's the perfect place to unburden their conscience—or at least say what's on their mind.

Yet how many times have you seen (or maybe experienced) complaining and gossiping about someone and—surprise!—the stall door opens and out walks the topic of conversation.

Years ago, I witnessed this in action. A colleague, "Ben," walked up to me while I was at the sink and started complaining about his boss and the fact that he was having a performance review that day. I tried to give Ben a couple nonverbal cues that someone else was in the bathroom, but he either didn't notice or didn't care. Right when Ben's complaints hit a real crescendo, the stall door opened and there was his boss.

"See you at two," the boss said to Ben as he exited quickly. Later that afternoon I found out what happened. "I thought I was done," Ben told me. "Turned out, it was the most meaningful performance review I've ever had. We really got the issues out on the table."

Ben was lucky—it could have gone the other way.

PERSONALITY OR BEHAVIOR?

Some people will rub you the wrong way because of their personality. Their style is different than yours—formal to your casual (or vice versa). Or maybe they have a habit that irks you—they hum in a monotone while they work in the next cubicle. They talk too much—like that "let me tell you about my crazy weekend" person who camps out at your desk first thing on Monday morning. Or they talk too little—like that person who always wears headphones and never interacts with anyone.

Behaviors, however, are an entirely different matter. They're all about how people treat and interact with others. Basically, behaviors fall into three categories. To illustrate, I'll use the analogy of a stoplight.

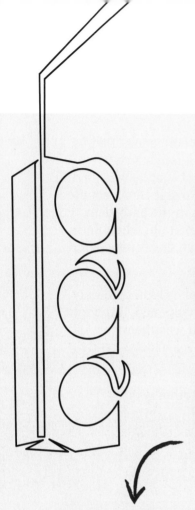

GREEN LIGHT Everyone is in sync and gets along. People enjoy collaborating. They're positive and encouraging of each other. It's rare—but if you find it then it's a green light all the way!

RED LIGHT If you encounter harassing or bullying behaviors, or if you feel unsafe or threatened in any way by a coworker, then you must escalate the matter immediately to your boss and to human resources. This is an intolerable situation and must be stopped.

YELLOW LIGHT The far larger and more common category is in between, with an array of behaviors and interactions that are problematic. Some you can shrug off, others must be addressed. Deciding how to address them is where the flashing caution light comes in. You need to discern how best to respond. Let's start with the two extremes.

GRIN AND BEAR IT.
This is not sustainable. One of these days, you're going to be so fed up, you'll probably overreact to the smallest provocation.

DISH THE DIRT RIGHT BACK. This Machiavellian approach of returning negative with more negative is toxic.

That leaves four alternatives in the middle.
Which one you pick, when, and why will depend on many factors, including the severity of the behavior, the people involved, the culture of your company, and your relationship with your boss and others around you. But in general, here are some guidelines to consider before you take any of these steps.

1 RAT TO YOUR BOSS.

If you've suffered an egregious affront of some kind, it may be time to bring a coworker's behavior to your boss's attention. But bringing your boss into it is like calling the police on the neighbors when they're having a loud party. The next day, they're still your neighbors, and things will never be the same. The same goes with telling your boss about what someone did to you. Your work relationship with that person will never be the same. It isn't that you shouldn't involve the boss, but be aware of the consequences.

2 PEER PRESSURE.

If you decide to confront a coworker in a group setting, be aware that this type of peer pressure usually backfires. The person will undoubtedly get defensive and complain that you're all ganging up on him or her. The only time this type of peer pressure works is to encourage positive behavior—for example, meeting in a group to decide how to tackle a project. Everyone in the group agrees to do a specific part, then that peer pressure is to perform—and people usually do. But peer pressure to stop doing something negative usually results only in drama.

3 GO TO A TRUSTED ADVISOR.

This might seem like a great idea. You confide in a colleague who promises to keep it between the two of you. Yet if you take this step, just make sure that the person you confide in at work is incredibly trustworthy and mature. Otherwise, you've just put the gossip mill on high speed. When the person gets wind of what you said (tell one person and you've told 20), you'll be accused of talking behind his or her back. And beware—people form cliques at work, just like they did in school. You could end up confiding in the wrong person.

4 SPEAK ONE-ON-ONE.

This takes some guts, but it may be your best bet. Immediately after the incident, tell your coworker what bothered you. Use "I" statements, not "you" statements, which can come across as accusatory. State your case, explain how you feel, and then listen for the response. It may be that your colleague was not aware of the impact of his or her actions. You could reach an understanding. If it persists, however, you will probably have to go to the boss about it.

SELF-INTEREST TO SHARED INTEREST: IT STARTS WITH YOU

The more discerning you become about why you and your colleagues clash, the better you'll become at managing interpersonal skills. If there's one upside to all this, it's that. Because the fact is, interpersonal relationships are challenging, and group dynamics amplify those challenges exponentially.

Put any group of people together and there's bound to be a variety of strong opinions; conflict over different choices and competing self-interests are to be expected. The ideal is for all those self-interests to become a shared interest—i.e., aligned with the mission and purpose of the organization or project. But that won't happen if people stay polarized from each other.

It's been said that the strength of a team is each individual member— and the strength of each individual member is the team. Given human nature, each coworker will have his or her own agenda and self-interest. Add personalities, pressure, stress, deadlines, and money, and the result can be a powder keg. So you've got to buy in to the concept of "collective genius," with the belief that a group can be stronger than any one individual. What brings that group together is a sense of shared purpose—"we're all in this together" to accomplish a common, overarching goal.

But interpersonal relationships are a two-way street. They begin with a whole new level of self-awareness. What in *you* sparks the conflict or fans the flame? You might be surprised at how much a subtle change in your behavior—such as listening more attentively to others—can make a major impact. It's all about your personal leadership, which can be developed at every level. These skills include self-awareness, self-control, motivation, empathy, and other interpersonal skills that constitute emotional intelligence (which we discuss more in depth in Chapter Six,

Social Creatures at Work

We're all social creatures, and research shows work friendships help us thrive at work. But be self-aware. Sharing from your personal life is fine, as it lets others get to know you. Oversharing (i.e., your dating life, or the latest drama with that annoying relative) can make others want to avoid engaging with you. What you say, in conversation as well as through nonverbal cues, can affect the way you're perceived by peers.

"Building Political Capital"). The more aware and emotionally intelligent you become, the more you become attuned to your own unconscious biases—which are preventing you from connecting with people who are different from you.

Remember, these are relationships, even though you may never be friends outside of work. These are the people you spend the bulk of your time with—whether in a physical office or connecting virtually. To have a relationship with them, you need to remember your **ACT**:

✔ BE AUTHENTIC
✔ FORGE A CONNECTION
✔ GIVE OTHERS A TASTE OF WHO YOU REALLY ARE

Your ACT can help you relate to others. When you let your guard down and show your genuine self, others will be more likely to do so as well. That allows you to connect with your colleagues, see them for who they are (including the strengths they bring to the team), and discover commonalities. Pets, kids, movies, music, favorite foods—even small things can build bigger bridges.

As you undertake this journey into greater self-awareness, here are ways to increase interpersonal relationships. These tips are so important, we call them the "Ten Commandments."

THE TEN COMMANDMENTS FOR DEALING WITH COWORKERS

1 **Thou shalt drop** your ego. Ego is not your amigo. You can't think you have the power to "fix" other people—or that the world would be a far better place if you were in charge.

2 **Thou shalt hit** the pause button. When you're triggered by something a coworker says or does, you can't react like a sprinter off the blocks. Pause between the stimulus and your reaction. Speak too fast and you'll regret it later. The ol' "counting to 10" maneuver can prevent you from saying or doing anything that only escalates the conflict. And that pause should be doubled if you're furiously thumbing an email or text to respond to their idiocy.

3 **Thou shalt remember** the Golden Rule. Treat others the way you want to be treated.

No, you aren't trying to get nominated for martyr of the year. But if you can show a little humility and remember your humanity (saying "good morning" or "thank you"), you'll be surprised how much negativity can be defused.

4 **Thou shalt make** others feel better after every interaction. Early in my career, someone gave me some amazing advice. People should always feel better after they've spoken with you— even if it's a difficult conversation. How? By focusing on the issues that need to be acknowledged, the problems that can't be ignored. Ask for and listen to the opinions of others.

5 **Thou shalt understand** others before being understood. Among Dr. Stephen Covey's 7 Habits of Highly Effective People, one of my favorites is "seek first to understand, then be understood." What makes others tick? What's important to them? What's their communication style? What are their strengths and weaknesses? View your coworkers through the lens of seeking to understand—instead of trying to make yourself understood.

6 **Thou shalt listen** twice as much as you speak. You have two ears and one mouth for a reason: listen twice as much as you speak. Listen to understand and take in information. Listen without interrupting—not waiting for the other person to take a breath so you can jump in. Don't rush to judge; ask questions if you don't understand.

7 **Thou shalt be open** to feedback. Are you part of the problem—or part of the solution? In almost any workplace conflict, you're on one side or the other. Maybe you didn't start it, but if you complain to any and all who will listen and play passive-aggressive games, you are escalating the problem. Do you say one thing but do another? These habits may be so ingrained, you may not even be aware of your own behaviors. Get feedback from a mentor or trusted advisor on how you might handle the challenge, especially if the conflict is with your boss.

8 **Thou shalt cease** the watercooler gripe sessions. A constant theme in watercooler conversation is talking about the boss or complaining about a coworker. *You're not going to believe what they said/did today!* Stop! What do you really get out of feeding the negativity? You're only escalating the stress for yourself and for everyone else. Unless there is a breach of ethics or integrity—in which case, this becomes a human resources issue—let it go and move on.

9 **Thou shalt assume** the better motive. Maybe they aren't really out to get you. Your boss gives you a last-minute assignment late on a Friday and needs it done by midday Monday. Your coworker announces there's a major problem, and suddenly you're dragged in to help solve it. Unfair? Maybe—maybe not. This happens all the time in organizations. Priorities shift and things escalate. Maybe the boss just got handed that assignment from on high. Maybe your coworker just uncovered a problem while it's still contained, before it becomes an even bigger issue. When in doubt, assume the better motive. You have to do the work anyway, so you might as well put a better spin on it.

CONTINUED

10 **Thou shalt ask** for and offer help. Virtually everyone is good at something, and chances are your colleagues have strengths that you lack and vice versa. As you work together on a joint project or team initiative, focus on what each person brings. The more clearly you can see your colleagues, the better you'll understand how to work with them. What help can you offer to get the job done? What help can you ask for? Working together, focused on a common problem, can help build bridges.

These Ten Commandments won't miraculously change your workplace relationships. But they will help you navigate the troubled waters.

COLLABORATING WITH SLACKER COWORKERS

It's a common scenario: it's 11 o'clock on a Thursday night, and you're scrambling to piece together a group presentation that's happening tomorrow. No one else is online; the last email reply you received was five hours ago. All evening you've been rewriting slides that you received yesterday, even though they should have been turned in a week ago. This, you think, is why teamwork is a nightmare. Remember how much you hated team projects in college? Well, things haven't changed much.

If this scenario resonates with you, you aren't alone. Research shows that nearly a quarter of workers put in extra time each week to make up for their "slacker" colleagues. What's worse, four out of five employees say that their work quality declines when they have to cover for a coworker.

If you seek to understand, you may look at the problem (and your coworkers) differently. Most of us want others to work the same way we do. But everyone has a different work style and contributes differently.

When you find yourself in the midst of that late-night scramble, ask what led to this imbalance in who's doing what:

Was your
communication unclear?

Was the work delegated to
others, or did you assign
yourself most of it?

Are others actually busy,
but maybe not as visibly
busy as you are?

Have you micromanaged
others (whether they report
to you or they are fellow
team members) to the point
they feel unmotivated?

Reflecting on these tough questions now can save you from repeating the problem in the future. If your self-examination turns up clean, it's important to have a conversation with the person who's causing the problem. The approach is everything here, and the best place to start is with more curiosity than blame. (Remember, use "I" statements, not "you" accusations.) For example, "I'm nervous that we aren't going to have this done on time because I don't have the information to work from," versus "You aren't delivering the information."

Many times, you'll find there's a reason this person hasn't been able to complete the work to your standards. With that information, you can have a productive conversation about how to tackle the current project and the next ones as well. If unacceptable coworker behavior continues, though, then it's time to involve your manager.

Lastly, keep in mind that good coworker connections make people more productive. When colleagues see each other as people, they are more engaged with each other and collaboration improves.

DEALING WITH STRESS— IT'S DIFFERENT FOR EVERYBODY

As business accelerates with faster, more frequent deadlines, stress also accelerates. Not everybody reacts to the same stresses. Among your coworkers, you may find people who "lose it" as soon as there is a hint of pressure, while others never seem to break a sweat. Instead of judging your coworkers' reactions to stress—*the boss just called a meeting in five minutes!*—understand that their reactions are just different than yours.

Daniel Goleman, in his extensive research and writing about emotional intelligence, advises that people are more likely to keep an open mind (and an even keel) if they get better at their own stress management. Here are some tips that may help:

✔ **GO** for a 10-minute walk outside the building.

✔ **REFLECT** on the root cause of your stress.

✔ **CONSIDER** alternative solutions or paths.

✔ **CONTEXTUALIZE** the moment in the whole of your life.

✔ **CALL OR TEXT** a friend you haven't spoken to in a while.

✔ **LOOK** at pictures of your loved ones.

✔ **IMMERSE** yourself in your favorite music, comedians, or online videos.

These simple steps can help you improve self-management and achieve "emotional balance"—improving your ability to handle anxiety, anger, and frustration. You may even find that, as your stress levels decrease, your annoying coworkers aren't so annoying anymore.

Forging that team dynamic requires mutual understanding and respect. Stop rushing to judge others or dismiss their ideas and suggestions. People aren't wrong in their thoughts or approaches—they're just different than you are. For example, you see differences in how your colleagues think and act. In your view, they waste too much time ruminating while you're very fast to act. These differences aren't a problem unless you make them a problem. Actually, differences strengthen the team—as long as the team is anchored in a common purpose. Your colleagues' ability to see all sides of a problem or situation is a definite plus, especially when combined with your fast decision-making.

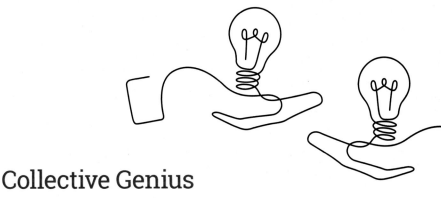

Collective Genius

Research shows that, in the early stages, teams composed of people who are all alike (homogenous) outperform those that are diverse. The reason is a lack of the disruption and conflict that can result when different perspectives, experiences, backgrounds, thinking, and communication styles are merged. But well-managed diverse teams significantly outperform well-managed homogenous teams over time.

When teams move from diversity to inclusion—where differences are not just tolerated but celebrated—they show strength in innovation and strategic thinking, and can leverage their differences to create collective genius.

CONFLICT MANAGEMENT

Last, but perhaps most important, we arrive at conflict—which most people want to avoid, even if that means simmering in resentment. Sure, conflicts that get out of hand can be corrosive. But conflict is also very healthy. It is only through conflict, quite frankly, that the best ideas are born. The problem, however, is that most people hate conflict so much, they'll go along just to get along. But that's an even bigger problem.

Your goal is to engage in constructive conflict. Use those moments of disagreement to ask the deeper questions—why and how. In discerning the opinions and rationales of others, you'll uncover more insights that come from having varied perspectives and experiences. This is constructive conflict at its best, embracing those moments of clashing opinions as opportunities to innovate.

GIVE TO GET. Not everything has to be your way. Everyone likes to win, but you need to know when to step aside or step down on minor points so that you create buy-in from others. If you appear to be steamrolling without giving thought to how others think or feel, the conflict will only escalate. When people "win" something, they'll be more likely to support you and the greater objective.

DON'T INFLATE THE PROBLEM. Avoid making sweeping judgments and statements like "We always have this problem!"

Instead, acknowledge where consensus and agreement exist. Then the disagreements won't appear to be so all-consuming. By isolating the conflicts, they can be more easily addressed without becoming part of an inflated problem.

KEEP YOUR COOL. Become self-aware about what you do and the behaviors you exhibit when you're about to lose your composure. Do you raise your voice, change your body posture, harden your facial expression, etc.? Others pick up on these cues, which puts them on the defensive. Stay neutral. Focus on the facts, and whatever you do, don't personalize the conflict.

LISTEN TO THE OTHER SIDE OF THE STORY. There are often many solutions to any problem, and almost every idea has some merit. Listen (don't just hear) when others explain their ideas. What can you learn? What elements of various ideas can be combined? Avoid impatience and jumping to conclusions too early in the process. Take time to really define the problem and hear people out.

TURN OFF THE JUDGMENT. Don't make assumptions about the value of people's ideas or contributions based on whether or not you like them. Your goal is to increase how valued people feel so that they'll be more empowered to speak up and share ideas. Diversity of thinking is one of the greatest resources any team can have.

Group dynamics are challenging because people are different. But part of those differences is having unique gifts, preferences, strengths, and styles of working. And that's a good thing! Creativity and innovation, which are the lifeblood of every organization, can only occur when people get out of their comfort zone. Often this happens when we challenge each other to "color outside the lines." So when you find yourself annoyed by a coworker and losing patience, ask yourself why. What's the lesson to be learned here about yourself and others? In the process, your interpersonal skills will improve. Then, as you shift, everyone else probably will as well. Strangers locked in conflict will become colleagues who respect their differences and see them as a source of strength.

YOUR 5 TAKEAWAYS

FOR DEALING WITH COWORKERS

Can't live without them, so purposefully live with them.

Ego is not your amigo. Maybe it's not them, it's you.

Don't judge; understand others before demanding to be understood.

Interpersonal relationships are a two-way street. Use your ACT: be *authentic*, make a *connection*, and give others a *taste* of who you are, not what you do.

Embrace (don't avoid) constructive conflict as the way to collective genius.

Chapter Six

BUILDING POLITICAL CAPITAL:

Forget the Org Chart

If you think about it, companies are a lot like families. There are spoken and unspoken rules of what's acceptable and what's not—for instance, whether it's OK to eat dinner in the living room, feet up on the coffee table, or if it's strictly "fine dining" at your house. Then there's the matter of conversation around the table, regarding topics that are strictly taboo. But if you're new to the family and don't know the culture, you could end up saying or doing the wrong thing—or worse yet, offending someone.

Organizations are no different, although the minefields to navigate go far beyond trying to chat up weird Uncle Bobby at Thanksgiving. Organizations are complex mazes of personalities, constituencies, issues, and rivalries. There are people with strong egos and those who are looking to amass their own power. Even when the boundaries are not that pronounced, people still like to build and defend their own "sandboxes"—no matter how small or large.

And forget that organizational chart. There are informal networks and unwritten rules about how things get done and by whom. You need to figure out who really has "the juice." The easiest way is to see who can spend the money. Who can hire and fire? And then there are those who have the power behind the scenes; they may not be as obvious at first—and it shifts! Think about the big boss's assistant, who controls both the calendar and the access. Ignore or dismiss that person at your peril! (Read on for a chilling example.) And then there's the person who operates way behind the scenes—nobody even knows his or her exact title or responsibilities. But this person's name is mentioned with a tone that's somewhere between awe and fear.

Swirling around are the power grabbers and the political operators. They're the ones who are trying to seize visibility and power (you

Q   There's no buy-in for my ideas, and I don't know how to get access to people who can help me. And if that weren't bad enough, I'm caught between my boss and my boss's boss. What am I doing wrong?

A   The problem is politics—but before you recoil from that word, understand that all organizations are political. It's how power and influence are channeled. You need to identify the "people who know people"—the gatekeepers and influencers who get things done. Use your emotional intelligence to read people, the politics, and how to gain access and influence.

can usually tell who they are by the names they drop). This doesn't happen everywhere to the same degree. But people being people—just as in that big extended family full of personalities and history—there will be cliques and alliances.

All of which might make the case for lying low— just staying out of the whole mess and doing your job. And some people claim they do. You hear them say with a little smugness, "Oh, I'm above all that. I get ahead on my own work." Maybe they do, but only in their heads. The truth is you can't advance your career—or come close to taking control of it—if you don't learn how to develop some political capital. You earn this through relationships with others, especially those above you, and this becomes a daily practice you can never ignore. The long-term benefits of having such capital can be amazing—just as the price of losing that capital suddenly because of a stupid slipup can be catastrophic.

The goal here is to become as politically savvy as you can—which should not be confused with being "political," usually code for not always being trusted by others. Being politically savvy means you can influence those around you (even above you), create buy-in, and get things done with others. And with people now changing jobs so often, this know-how is another must-have you'll carry along in your toolbox as you go from one job, one culture, to the next.

YOU CAN'T ADVANCE YOUR CAREER IF YOU DON'T DEVELOP SOME POLITICAL CAPITAL.

To get to this place, we need to spend this chapter looking at office politics through two lenses. First, we'll explore the *skills* you need to discern and operate within any environment. Second, we'll learn about the *people* you need to work well with, from your boss to your boss's boss to the "influencers"—in other words, the networked web of relationships in any organization.

YOUR POLITICAL SAVVY

Let's start with you—your skills—because you'll never succeed if you don't have self-awareness of how you are perceived and how you can more effectively interact with others.

The first step is to understand the environment you're in. You may work for a company that prides itself on having few titles and even fewer layers. Good ideas can come from anywhere, and every voice gets to be heard. That's great, but don't kid yourself. The world is ripe with hierarchy.

Even in a flat organization, which appears to be so nonhierarchical, you need to understand who has influence and who doesn't. Who can expedite or stonewall things? This is all part of learning to become "emotionally intelligent" (as we will cover later).

If you're new to a company or you've joined a new team, this will take some figuring out. Even if you've been around for a few years, things may have shifted because of other changes, such as a new boss or boss's boss. Promotions, transfers, teams expanding or contracting—all of it changes the dynamics. And since you're probably a career nomad who

THE INFORMAL NETWORK

THE INFLUENCERS. It sounds like a good title for a spy movie. But these aren't the bad guys. On the contrary, within any organization there are key players who get things done. And they don't operate alone. They rely on and align with others to expedite things. How do you identify them?

FOLLOW THE MONEY. Who controls the flow of resources? Who are the major gatekeepers for information and decision-making? Get to know the guides and helpers who are part of the networks of the movers and shakers. Seek to become part of their network by being known for who you are and what you can contribute.

makes a change every few years, with each new job you'll need to read the tea leaves all over again.

Every organization has them: the "politicizers" who seek power, grab attention, and curry favor for their own ends—and at everyone else's expense. They can kill culture and drag down performance. Be aware of these characters, and don't become one yourself!

POLITICIZER BINGO BOARD

The Backstabber	The Credit-Seeker	The Name-Dropper	The Schmoozer	The Gossip
The Finger-Pointer	The Saboteur	The Kiss-Up	The Two-Face	The Shape-Shifter
The BSer	The Operator	The Spy	The Yes-Man	The Egomaniac
The Informer	The Favorite	The Power-Grabber	The Anointed	The Entitled

EI: DON'T GO ANYWHERE WITHOUT IT

To be politically savvy, you need an all-important skill that will serve you well throughout your career: *emotional intelligence.* You need to be emotionally intelligent for many reasons related to your advancement—from getting along with your boss, to managing and motivating others, to relating to people across cultures and context. In this discussion of discerning and navigating office politics, you can't survive without emotional intelligence.

Emotional intelligence is the ability to identify, understand, and manage your own emotions and to read and understand the emotions of others. It's composed of empathy, adaptability, self-awareness, and similar competencies. Research suggests that emotional intelligence (EI) is twice as important as cognitive ability (better known as IQ) in predicting performance.

Daniel Goleman, the author of *Emotional Intelligence*—who works closely with our firm—considers EI to be more important than ever. As he wrote in his groundbreaking best seller: "I envision a day when emotional intelligence will have become so widely understood that we need not mention it because it has melded with our lives. . . . Likewise, EI qualities such as self-awareness, managing destructive emotions, and empathy would be givens in the workplace, 'must-haves' for being hired and promoted, and most especially for leadership."

Given Goleman's vision for just how potent EI is in the workplace, it's clear you need to develop it, particularly when navigating office politics. Here are a few EI tips to raise your profile and advance in your career:

WHO'S ON FIRST?

Notice where in the room the power is—and don't assume it's with the boss. It may be a star performer or a group of people who are closely aligned with the boss. Where are the alliances and where are the factions? This will tell you whose ideas are more likely to garner support—and whose support you'll need for your own ideas. Also, be on the lookout for those who always seem to know what's going on, and whom others go to for advice. These are the tracings of the networks that exist within teams, departments, and companies. You'll want to know where they are, who's on them, and how you can join. You need to align yourself with the decision-makers and influencers who can put a word in for you on that job in a different department or that bigger assignment. And when there's a task force or cross-department initiative, they'll want you to be part of the team. You can't push it, but the higher your performance, the more you'll get noticed.

THE CONTAGION FACTOR.

Team members, particularly leaders, can transmit their feelings, positive or negative, to others. If you're emotionally self-aware and send more positive feelings than negative ones, you can make a big improvement in the team dynamic. You don't have to be the team Pollyanna. But you can radiate more positivity than negativity. A can-do attitude may be cliché, but it works. Let's say you know the next team meeting or project update is bound to result in a debate. How might your colleagues react? What are your own feelings? How can you engage in the discussion in a way that turns opposing views into constructive conflict that yields meaningful discussion?

BE "PEOPLE SENSITIVE."

Learning to read people is a great skill, and it will serve you well in your career. You'll need your best observation skills. How do people react to stress, challenges, opportunities, and failure? See beyond the behaviors to the motivation that's driving those behaviors. How do people act in meetings? What are formal and informal conversations like? The more you can read the people around you, the better you can adjust your approach to influence others.

LEARNING
EMOTIONAL
INTELLIGENCE

Early in your career, your focus was on developing your technical skills. In fact, most of your training and development was of a technical nature—what you needed to do to get the job done (see Chapter Twelve, "Tapping Your Right Brain"). But Goleman stresses that emotional intelligence must be developed as soon as possible, even by young workers who don't understand the importance of this skill set. The difference in perception is pretty shocking: In a survey of 450 HR leaders, 92 percent saw emotional and social skills as crucial for being competitive in a global economy. But nearly 70 percent of recent graduates said those soft skills would get in the way, and they could succeed without them. Now, here's the wake-up call: if those new workforce entrants aren't socially and emotionally competent, they'll undermine their potential to become high performers.

So how do you learn emotional intelligence? A good place to start is by reading about it—Goleman has several books and writes frequently on the topic for the Korn Ferry Institute (*www.kornferry.com/institute*). Plus, there are ways you can develop and practice your emotional intelligence. Like any skill set, it takes awareness and practice.

FIND EI ROLE MODELS

It's a fact—people who exemplify emotional intelligence are more likely to inspire it in others. So who do you consider to be emotionally intelligent—good at reading others' emotions and in control of their own emotions and reactions? Observe that person in action. What attitudes and actions should you adopt to increase your EI?

ASK FOR EI FEEDBACK

As with any skill, you'll get better with feedback. Ask your boss or a colleague who is strong in emotional intelligence for their feedback on how you're doing. The best follow-up is right after a situation in which you showed (or should have displayed) emotional intelligence. What went well and what could have gone better?

SET EI FOR THE TEAM

Teams can help each other develop emotional intelligence. In fact, there should be an EI norm for the team: this is how we work together, interact, respect each other's views and emotions, and engage in discussions when opinions and views differ. These EI norms, such as shared self-awareness and open communication, can support collaboration and high performance.

CHECK INTO EI TRAINING

Your company may offer training in EI and related skills, such as listening and empathy. Ask the HR department—there may be online learning modules you can access.

BUILDING YOUR POLITICAL CAPITAL

Political capital is like any other kind of capital. It must be accrued over time. It's depleted the more you spend it, and you have to replenish it regularly. The amount of political capital you have depends on the amount of trust others have in you.

As I said earlier, knowing how to build it is crucial for the career nomad, who must transfer this skill set from job to job. At the same time, it's tricky to build any political capital if you're gone in two years—even if you stay for four years. Trust is time-dependent. It's a simple fact that the longer people know you and the more opportunities they have to interact with you, the more opportunities you have to build trust. The only way to expedite that process is by your actions and your performance.

Trust comes down to keeping your word. Watch your say/do ratio— if it isn't 1:1, your political capital won't grow. And when you need to build capital quickly, doing what you say you will do (and frequently exceeding expectations) is crucial. Just as building trust can be accelerated by the good you do, it can also be destroyed by missteps and poor choices. If you are told something in confidence, keep it that way. If you must discuss something, don't associate names with it.

Trust can also come through bonding. You were part of a team that handled a difficult project, or even a crisis. You were really in the trenches together. You may even bond over common interests—for example, you both volunteered for or participated in a fund-raiser for a cause that's personal and important to both of you. It goes without saying: your passion for the cause must be authentic.

When you have amassed political capital, you can spend it to further your goals, such as getting help to land that assignment you want or an introduction to someone higher up in the organization, or even assistance in tackling a problem that's bigger than you realized. But don't overestimate the amount of political capital you have, and constantly replenish it. Reciprocity is a real thing: you need to give to get, always being consistent in your performance and showing high integrity in your actions.

The Trusted Friend

Some of the greatest friendships in life are forged in the workplace. You never know where they may come from; you work on the same project together, or maybe you both like the same sports team. Ironically, it may come from working for a bad boss—great friendships often can be forged between coworkers enduring the same nightmare.

No matter how they're formed, the most effective work friendships are those that aren't broadcast. They don't high-five each other or post themselves together on Facebook. That allows one friend to try to pull levers for the other and reduces claims of favoritism if one moves up the ladder later. Trust is, of course, the critical bond between them, and nothing is sadder than when that trust is broken between them. Seek to establish these bonds in your career; nurture them, and never betray them.

AVOIDING
POLITICAL BACKLASH

Now that you've built all this political capital, especially with your boss, you don't want to diminish it—or worse yet, lose it—because of an unwise move. It's not about playing it safe. Taking no risks is a real risk and may single you out as someone who can't take on a bigger job or broader responsibilities. Most companies today encourage risk-taking, creativity, and pushing boundaries. Even failure is embraced—as long as failure happens fast and the learning happens even faster. (Psychologists refer to this as having "psychological safety"—meaning you won't be punished if you make a mistake.)

But unless you're among the rare disrupters—Elon Musk or the late Steve Jobs, who rocked their companies and their industries—you need to figure out how to do this. For 99 percent of us, it will mean getting buy-in, starting with your boss. First (and no surprise here), you need to apply your emotional intelligence. How does your company react to the new and different? Consider what happened to the last person who tried a new idea that didn't work out. Is that person still there? How did the organization respond? Were more resources brought in to help problem-solve and strategize? Or did people run for the corners while waiting to see who was thrown under the bus?

Once you understand how your organization (read: your boss) handles risk-taking, you can decide how to present new ideas or push back on "how we've always done things." Rather than jumping into the deep end with no life preserver, it's probably more politically astute to wade in. Test the waters, see if you're likely to sink or swim, and then go in a little deeper.

FLOAT THE IDEA. Let's say you've got an idea for a new approach, a better way of doing things, or another way to attack the problem. It may be an innovation. Or you may be trying to overturn what your boss wants to do or how things have always been done. These are all political moves because they test conventional wisdom and depart from the tried-and-true. People are usually averse to change, which means it's better to start by floating the idea, especially with your boss. Your objective is to start the conversation and plant the idea in your manager's head. If you get the green light, then off you go! But what if the response is lukewarm at best or an outright rejection? If your boss has the final say on everything, then hearing no at the outset probably killed your idea (at least for now). If you keep pushing it, you won't get anywhere and could end up hurting yourself.

WADE IN DEEPER. If you get or feel some leeway, however, you may be able to keep the idea alive. When there is a chance to maneuver, take a step into deeper water. But don't go on your own say-so. You need evidence—that means research and real data—to back up your plan. If you go to your boss with real facts, you're more likely to get buy-in, and your boss is more likely to support you.

GET YOUR PEERS ON BOARD. As we discussed in Chapter Five, "Coping With Coworkers," positive peer pressure works. One person makes (or pushes for) a positive change and then others start to join him or her. Then the majority rules—the more people who get behind this new idea or approach, the more likely others will come along.

TAKE THE PLUNGE. This won't happen often, but there may be times when you go all in—committing yourself to pushing ahead no matter what—especially if enough of your peers are with you. Take the example of a boss who suggested his team move office locations; for some, the relocation would mean doubling their commutes. The team got together and pushed back against the idea. They weren't going to go! The boss, who wasn't heavy-handed and was known for giving employees a fair amount of autonomy, backed down and decided not to pursue the location change.

The Digital
Deadly Sins

Digital communication is like breathing—it's second nature and you can't survive without it. The sheer volume and frequency of emails and texts make it easy to fire off a note or reply without thinking. Do that at your peril. Careers have been ruined by emails!

Here are some of the biggest and most deadly sins of digital communication and what to be aware of.

THAT "PRIVATE" EMAIL JUST GOT FORWARDED.
You assumed the email you wrote to one person—badmouthing the boss, making fun of colleagues, complaining about other departments—was never going to be seen by anyone else. But there it is, circulating around the department, and now your boss wants to talk to you. Always remember: anyone can forward anything—and that includes texts too!

YOUR "OK" JUST GOT SOMEONE MAD.
So much of communication isn't what you say but how you say it, and that's the problem with digital: emails and texts have no context. You don't have a tone of voice, as with phone conversations. You don't have verbal and nonverbal cues, as when you're in person. Emails and texts land flat. Take the response "OK," for example. Is that begrudging? Agreeable? Enthusiastic? Can't tell—and someone's assumption may not match your intention.

YOUR 😊😊😊 IS GETTING RIDICULOUS.
I'm always amazed by how many emails and texts I receive, including in business, that are populated with emoji. I once received a message with a bizarre expression that had me puzzled. Was that a smile,

136

a frown, or a gas bubble? I don't know, you tell me:

Don't overuse these little faces—and don't expect them to speak for you.

YOU GOT YOUR BOBS MIXED UP. There's Bob, your friend. And then there's Bob, your boss's boss. In your haste, you didn't double-check the auto-filled email address before hitting send. Then a sick feeling come over you. In your sent emails, you've written a gripe manifesto with (count 'em) three expletives, and it's sitting in the wrong Bob's email inbox.

YOU SENT AN EMAIL IN ANGER. Never, ever a good idea. The more riled up you are, the more time you need to respond. One way is to write it all out in an email *without* any address on it and then delete it! Now that you have it out of your system, write a second email. Save it to drafts. Reread it a few times and then—if you're sure it isn't going to backfire on you—hit send.

YOU DIDN'T PROOFRE@D YOUR EMAIL. The occasional typo is one thing, but multiple misspellings, obvious grammatical mistakes, and dropped words make you look sloppy (or worse). It's also a sign of disrespect to the recipient(s). Having a tagline that reads "Siri didn't proofread this for me" isn't an excuse! Read it back to yourself, preferably aloud.

YOU CC THE ENTIRE ORG CHART. Does everyone really have to be on that email? Transparency is one thing, but too many ccs makes you look either naive or overly self-promotional. Be discreet about the number of people you cc and bcc on your emails.

YOU REPLY ALL, ALL THE TIME. If there's one thing that will get on people's nerves, it's the worthless reply all that's sent to 17 people, 17 times. (You know the kind: Great job! Great idea! Got it!) Do everyone a favor and reply—but not to all.

YOU THINK RECALLING YOUR MESSAGE ERASES IT FROM THE PLANET. If you think recalling an email will right all of your wrongs or be your lifeline to safety, guess again. It rarely works. And, human nature being what it is, when people receive a recall on an email, they can't wait to find the original and see how you screwed up.

YOU TRY TO SOLVE THE PROBLEMS OF THE WORLD IN AN EMAIL. Just because you have as much space as you want to write in that email, don't. Digital communication should be concise. If you have that much to say, pick up the phone.

THE POLITICAL
PEOPLE

Now that you've explored your political skills, we can take the next step of understanding the people side of politics. No matter how flat the organization, you have a boss and your boss has a boss. This is potentially the most politically charged relationship you'll have to navigate from the earliest days in your career.

You may be trying to impress your boss's boss in hopes of opening some doors for yourself (without looking like you're gunning for your boss's job). Or you may be put on the spot—in a meeting, on a conference call, or in a hallway conversation—about how "things" are going. That supposedly casual comment is a double-edged sword.

Getting caught between your boss and the boss's boss is not only uncomfortable, it puts you at risk. (Remember, pawns are important in chess, but they get sacrificed, too.) To the best of your ability, get a reading on that relationship. Do your boss and the big boss get along? You know the statistic: people hate their bosses about half the time. Is there friction between them, whether personally or professionally? Tune in to the grapevine so you can gather intelligence as to what's going on and how wise or risky it is to stay aligned with your boss.

The challenge for you is that it's hard to keep the big picture in perspective when suddenly you're being singled out by the boss's boss. The attention is flattering, and you know it's important to advancing your career. But before you rush to offer an opinion, position yourself as an expert, or maneuver into the spotlight, you need to understand the political context: Why is your boss's boss engaging you all of a sudden? Most importantly, what's the implication of anything you say? These are not casual interactions. So what do you do? There are five basic choices:

1 You're Teflon. You're too scared to say anything that will stick to you or alienate anyone, so you just mumble a little non-specific information. Maybe you dodged a bullet in the moment, but the risk is you just showed that you're spineless and clueless.

2 Repeat what's known. You stick to the script of the last team meeting. *We're on target with X and Y, but Z is taking longer than we thought.* This feels like the safest option, but the risk is the boss's boss could still press you for further details—and your opinion.

3 Give your opinion. You not only offer an assessment or update, you also give your opinion of what you think should happen. *The problem is X, and the sooner we address that the better.* You take this political risk because you want to impress the boss's boss. But be prepared for the big boss to repeat everything you said and attribute it to you. The upside is you may ingratiate yourself with the big boss, but the downside is you risk alienating your boss because you deviated from his or her thinking.

4 Defend your boss. You put the best possible spin on things. *It's going really well. We got over the bumps, and it's all on track.* You do this out of a sense of loyalty to your boss. And if it's true, that's great. But if it isn't, then you've just lied to the boss's boss and aligned yourself with your boss, who from the sounds of it could be out sooner rather than later (and perhaps you, too).

5 Throw your boss under the bus. In giving your opinion, you openly criticize your boss. (This is the riskiest of all political moves—proceed with caution!) *Between us* (warning: there's no such thing), *the problems are a lot bigger than anyone admits.* The reason is you want the boss's boss to see not only your worth but also your boss's incompetence. You're also positioning yourself as being better in that role—and the big boss knows it, which may or may not work out for you.

So how should you answer? In truth, there is no formulaic approach here. There may be times when a nonanswer really is your best response. This is usually the case when you're at a lower level in an organization, with no influence and no real insight. (The boss's boss knows this but is probably digging for anything you might have heard.) And there are times when you should absolutely distance yourself from your boss, especially when the boss is doing a bad job of managing things and failure is all but guaranteed.

Whichever way you answer, you have to understand what's really being asked and the political implications of your response. No matter how flat the organization, with this conversation you just jumped right over your boss's head.

WHO HIRED YOUR BOSS?

This is a political point you can't afford to miss: Was your boss hired or inherited? It makes a significant difference to what happens to your boss and how you should answer when asked to give feedback on any project or on your boss.

If the big boss inherited your boss from a previous leader, then your boss could very well be on shaky ground. The big boss may question the boss's abilities or allegiance. While you should never bad-mouth anyone for your own gain, if the big boss wants to bring in his or her own lieutenant, your boss is probably on the way out. If performance is an issue, the boss will be gone sooner rather than later, and maybe you along with him or her.

If the big boss hired your boss, that indicates a much closer relationship and probably longevity for your boss. This may be true even if your boss is a mediocre performer. Anything short of complete incompetence or malfeasance will be excused. Your boss is going to stay, so dismiss any thoughts you have of taking over that job. It isn't going to happen. (And when you see your boss and your boss's boss head off to lunch together, you just got your confirmation.)

THE MOST INFLUENTIAL PEOPLE YOU NEVER WANT TO SNUB

Guess who? Where your mind goes first is a window into your political savvy. If you immediately went to senior leadership, you're thinking hierarchically—bigger title, more influence. But that's too obvious and, frankly, not that politically savvy. At the top of the list of the most influential people you never want to snub is that senior leader's assistant. Part gatekeeper, part right hand, the assistant is in a position of high trust. A good (or bad) word about you from the assistant to the boss could help (or hurt) your chances of advancing in your career.

The same goes for receptionists, who are on the front line of everyone who goes into and out of an office. When interview candidates come into the office, many hiring managers will ask the receptionist for feedback on how they acted. Were they pleasant? Did they make conversation? Or were they rude and dismissive?

Ken Blanchard, an acclaimed management expert and best-selling author of several books, including *The One Minute Manager*, shared a story with me about a pilot who was applying for a job at another airline. Now, this was a very experienced pilot with the kind of skills any airline would be glad to have. But on the flight to where the airline was based, the pilot was rude to the crew. At corporate headquarters, the pilot was dismissive of not one but two receptionists who greeted him. One of the receptionists called HR and reported everything, including the tip-off from the flight crew about the pilot's bad behavior. The upshot? The pilot was sent home without ever getting the interview.

So now who do you think are the most influential people you never want to snub? If you said *everyone and anyone*, you got that right. Never assume that someone with a seemingly unimpressive title doesn't have influence and access. There are people behind the scenes whom senior leaders rely on for everything from institutional knowledge to accomplishing the seemingly impossible. These are the people you need to identify and align yourself with.

YOUR 5 TAKEAWAYS

FOR MASTERING OFFICE POLITICS

Forget the org chart—it's useless. Become a student of informal networks. These webs of relationships, formed by people to get work done, thread through company culture.

Identify the influencers who can expedite or stonewall things.

Exercise your emotional intelligence to build alliances.

Build your political capital on trust—it is earned, not given to you.

Never, ever underestimate the influence and political power that rests behind the scenes, with people whose titles may not "impress" you.

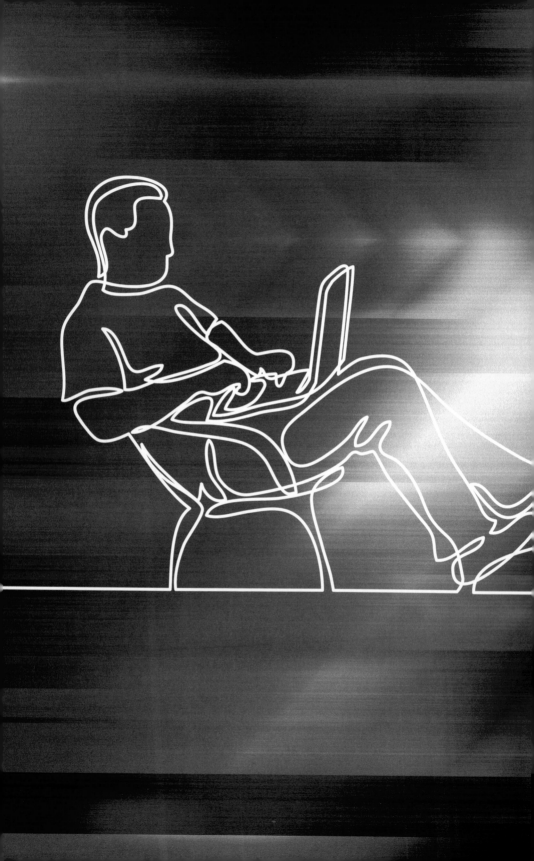

Chapter Seven

WORKING VIRTUALLY:

The Risks of Being Out of Sight

If you think about it, the virtual-work movement has created a whole new species, once as rare as snow leopards but now multiplying like uncaged rabbits. If you aren't one of them already, you surely have seen them. Denizens of coffeehouses, or really anywhere with a chair, Wi-Fi, and a power outlet, they'll be encamped for hours behind laptops, oddly talking to no one until you realize they're wearing earbuds. A 2 percent battery reading is the kiss of death for them, second only to loud noises, which send virtual workers scampering away like Dracula from light. They think they're harmless, but anyone who's bought coffee and then had to stand or leave has experienced the inconvenience. For their part, businesses are so worried about virtual workers soaking up space that they now keep background music louder in a fruitless effort to shoo them away.

JUST THE LACK OF COMMUTING TIME CAN BE SOUL-SAVING.

I say all this to make an important point: without a doubt, a lot of us would prefer to work virtually. Just the lack of commuting time can be soul-saving, and the benefit to your family life is immeasurable. And without all the distractions of the office, you're bound to get a lot more done. But at no point should you forget that being part of this species is by its very nature— at least potentially—a real irritant. Indeed, most people I know who work virtually are amazingly grateful for all the freedom they have, and just as amazingly ignorant about how others who *don't* have that freedom feel. They tend to lose sight of the fact that, while they're Skyping into a meeting, their

Q My new job allows me to work virtually. I can ditch my long commute, get more work done without distractions, and maybe get to the gym more often. Is there any downside?

A Don't kid yourself. You're right about all the upsides, but even though working virtually is on the rise, it's still far from the norm. That means you'll need to win over all those who still have to schlep into work. And while you may find yourself getting more done at home, will anyone know who you really are versus what you do?

faces happily framed by a comfy pillow, some poor person is sitting at that same meeting in person, stuck in a sterile conference room and still recovering from a two-hour traffic jam. And that poor person may be not only their colleague but also their boss or their boss's boss. This, in my mind, is a critical challenge to working virtually—somehow navigating the potential for resentment.

By the way, here's something else you probably haven't realized: if you aren't working virtually yet, you can expect that you will be during a significant part of your career. Polls show that the ranks of those working remotely have doubled in the United States in a decade, and that nearly half the workforce works virtually some or all of the time. As companies try to save on real estate, improve gender disparity, and keep shifting to the gig economy, this won't be the precocious perk it currently is— the kind that people negotiate and beg for today. More companies will embrace it, increasing the odds that as you move from job to job or take up contracting, you'll be home for part of your career—and, in the process, inhabiting surroundings very different from Planet In-Office.

This brings me to a favorite acronym of mine that is part and parcel of any successful career. If you are working virtually, you need to be **SEEN**. *Show* that you can be productive anywhere, *engage* with your boss and team, *enter* the office strategically, and *never* forget where you are when you're on calls with your boss, your boss's boss, and clients or customers. The more you are SEEN, the more successful you will be when working virtually.

S → Show that you can be productive

E → Engage with your boss and team

E → Enter the office strategically

N → Never forget where you are

S → SHOW THAT YOU CAN BE PRODUCTIVE ANYWHERE

Your untethered bliss is bound to cause some resentment. Part of the issue, perhaps the biggest, is just trying to convince people you are working at all, especially if it is a new arrangement. Your boss may be especially nervous about this, and your colleagues may be as well, out of fear of having to pick up your load. Of course, you may be logged in to collaboration software that shows everyone you're online, creating a baseline of built-in visibility. But if you're working on that report for eight straight hours with hardly a break, you could appear to be "off the radar."

The bottom line: performance says it all. Whether you're working in the next cubicle or in a cabin in the woods, what matters most is how well you do the work that needs to be done and stay focused on your boss's short-term goals and priorities.

To be productive while working virtually, you need to manage your time as well as your environment. These are table stakes for being productive. Some factors, like having Wi-Fi, almost seem quaint given the technological explosion of the past few years. Others are timeless, seemingly obvious conventions that deserve a brief refresher:

MANAGE DISTRACTIONS.
It's such a nice day—you tell yourself you can get in a quick nine holes of golf and then work later this evening. Or your new puppy is so cute playing with that old sock—you just have to post a video on Instagram. More mundane, there's nothing in the refrigerator and the laundry is piling up. Your spouse/partner thinks that, since you're working from home, you should be able to run the neighborhood car pool. Remember, working virtually means exactly that—working, just someplace other than the office. You're going to need rules and boundaries for yourself and others in your life. If you're a full-time employee working virtually, you need to be in sync with the office. Would you get up from your desk in the middle of the afternoon to do errands? Probably not. So don't do that when you're working virtually. If your boss calls you midday and you're at the gym, you'll send the wrong message.

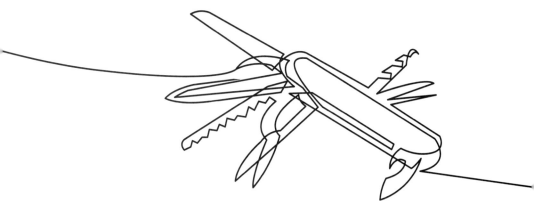

REMEMBER, THEY CAN HEAR YOU. Today's cell phones and headsets are super sensitive for picking up sound. They can detect that distinctive clunk of the microwave door closing and the faint beep-beep as you push the timer buttons. (Your colleagues on the line know it must be getting near lunchtime at your house.) The real offender, though? I've been on the phone with remote workers at least five times where I've heard the toilet flush in the background. Really? Biological needs or not, I just don't need to hear that. That little microphone isn't just picking up your voice, but everything (and I mean everything) that's going on around you. Just the other day, I was on a previously scheduled call with three other people to review customer activity. We had our spreadsheets open and were going over the details when I heard in the background, "Hey, did you pick up any wine?" Really. I guess it's always five o'clock somewhere.

KEEP TABS ON YOUR SURROUNDINGS. Skype truly is the next best thing to being there—not only for voice communication but also for visual. You can see others, just as they can see you in your surroundings. Just be mindful what's in view.

I remember interviewing someone who had a very large bottle of what looked like hard liquor on his desk—it turned out to be iced tea, but what a distraction from our conversation! And when you're on that all-important call with senior management or clients, make sure the door stays shut and the kids and the dog stay out. (Check out YouTube for a BBC live Skype interview with a geopolitical expert whose young child hilariously bursts into the room. The interview went viral, but for all the wrong reasons.)

DON'T GET STOPPED AT THE FIREWALL. This can't be emphasized enough. Technology will not be your friend and can often be a nightmare. Unfortunately, remote workers are often second tier when corporate IT rolls out the latest software upgrades. And if that isn't bad enough, firewalls meant to protect the company can keep you out. Some professionals, for example in engineering or design, require access to shared documents, many of them confidential. Make sure you can navigate the remote access to shared drives and documents, and that you have the safety and security protocols in place to protect sensitive or confidential information.

Lights, Camera, Action!

Have you asked a friend lately to tell you how you look on Skype? Or dared to see a screenshot of yourself? It's probably worse than you can imagine. Desk lamps create skin tones that suggest the onset of measles. The angle of those tiny laptop cameras can give even fashion models double chins. Bags under the eyes seem to be sagging with weights. The list goes on and on.

And yet—and this is a hard fact to swallow—the only image some of your colleagues may ever have of you is through this form of visual communication. I've read one blog post after another on how to deal with Skype appearance, and generally they can be helpful. But unless you're going to invest in an Oscar-winning makeup artist for every Monday-morning WebEx meeting, you're just going to have to spend considerable time doing tests and retests with patient friends and coworkers on what looks and sounds even remotely tolerable.

E → ENGAGE WITH YOUR BOSS AND TEAM

Face it, when you're working remotely you won't have the team building that happens in the moment, from spontaneous group lunches to discussions in the break room, which make up the social side of engagement. You can dial in for every session, but you won't be part of that casual meeting-after-the-meeting that happens in the hallway or when the boss drops by to discuss something.

It isn't that your boss and your colleagues are purposely trying to exclude you (avoid that paranoia), or that you won't be asked to come in

for certain meetings. But when you work off-site, you can't count on that office kismet that occurs when you and your boss show up in the kitchen at the same time and you start brainstorming about the latest project or a new opportunity. You can't be offended by what you're missing because you're not there.

You need to find other ways to engage, and that's going to mean communicating digitally—email and text—as well as telephonically. How and when? You and your boss are going to have to work that out. Your boss may be a big texter—or may never send a text. Your boss may want to discuss everything by phone or may prefer the brevity of email. Whatever form of communication works for you and your boss, make sure that you stay engaged with transparency and regularity.

Don't wait for the boss to initiate the conversation. You need to be proactive and update your boss frequently and continually on what you've accomplished and what you're currently working on. Until both you and your boss are in sync with this virtual arrangement, you may have to overshare the details. Otherwise, a day without any contact with your boss becomes two days, becomes a week, and then becomes a problem.

When you want to brainstorm with a colleague or your boss, reach out for a time to talk. But don't be on the phone constantly, like you're that homesick kid at camp. You might find that your colleagues will start avoiding your calls. This takes self-awareness about what you need and emotional intelligence about what suits your team. It's a balancing act that you have to discern and manage.

Will Working Virtually Hurt Your Chances of Being Promoted?

This is a tough one, because so many people do work virtually and that number is growing. But if you're known as the "work-from-home person," it could be difficult to overcome that perception. People may make assumptions that you are not leadership material. You'll be labeled as an individual contributor, and at some point your career will hit a wall. Unless your entire company is wired for managers and leaders to work virtually, you need to be aware. It may ultimately come down to unplugging from your home office and reconnecting physically with the company.

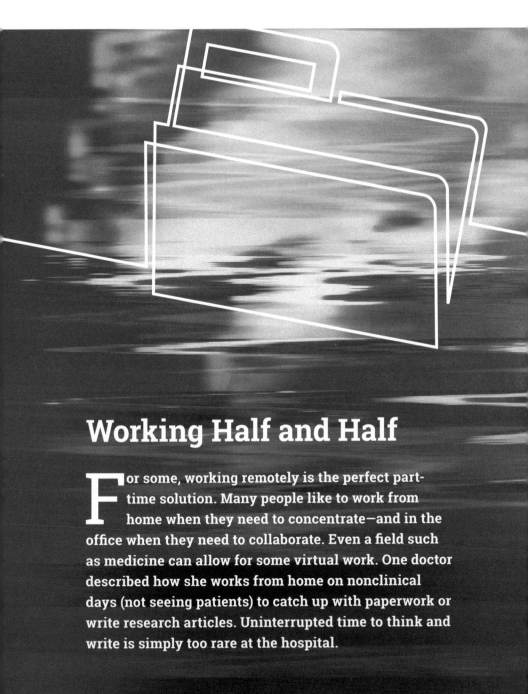

Working Half and Half

For some, working remotely is the perfect part-time solution. Many people like to work from home when they need to concentrate—and in the office when they need to collaborate. Even a field such as medicine can allow for some virtual work. One doctor described how she works from home on nonclinical days (not seeing patients) to catch up with paperwork or write research articles. Uninterrupted time to think and write is simply too rare at the hospital.

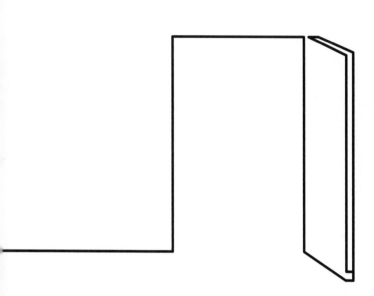

E → ENTER THE OFFICE STRATEGICALLY— DON'T BE "OUT OF SIGHT, OUT OF MIND"

Long before FaceTime became an Apple app and the preferred verb for mobile video chat, it was sage advice in the workplace. If you were, say, a sales rep who traveled extensively, you made sure to put in face time at the office so you didn't fall victim to being "out of sight, out of mind." Years ago, when people who worked largely on the road would return to the office—sometimes after being gone for weeks at a time—it was like reuniting with a long-lost relative. *So good to see you! How long has it been?*

Granted, digital communication today makes it far easier to stay in touch and be top of mind; there you are, in the boss's email inbox and on that string of text messages. And Skype can keep you close, but as we've mentioned, it just isn't the same as being in the office. There's a kind of chemistry that happens when people sit in the same room and start talking. Collective genius is born.

So one trick of learning how to work outside the office is to learn when to return to it, strategically. It may be for that monthly team meeting. Or perhaps you work remotely near a regional office and the CEO is coming to town—of course you should be there. You need to be part of that casual town-hall discussion with the CEO. But this isn't just about bosses. You need to engage with your teammates, spend some quality face time— lunch or coffee together—to see and hear them. When you're brainstorming a new project, you want to be there in person, if at all possible.

And don't forget your office manners. You may be used to exercise clothes and flip-flops, but now you have to put on real shoes. But don't overdress, as if you're on your first trip to the big city with a price tag still dangling from your new jacket. You should be able to enter and exit the office environment with ease, showcasing how you still fit in with everyone.

N → NEVER FORGET WHERE YOU ARE FOR IMPORTANT CALLS

Let's put it this way, a bad phone connection or intolerable background noise can ruin your career. I'm not talking about that impromptu call—your boss calls you with a quick question just as you're boarding your flight. I'm talking about that call you know is going to happen.

As a remote worker, you may sit at your favorite coffee shop in the morning. If you have a more casual working relationship with your boss, it may be just fine to pick up the phone there despite the chatter and music. But that isn't the case for an hour-long call, when the background noise may boom into everyone else's earbuds.

And for goodness' sake, remember how much your setup risks

resentment: background noise or Skype images of you in a T-shirt remind people about the sweet deal you have that they don't. Never underestimate the jealousy factor, especially when you're counting on those colleagues as "office allies" to keep you in the loop about what's going on, who's coming in, and when you ought to put in an appearance.

It's also important to be extra careful about maintaining a professional manner on these calls. I notice that remote workers, who don't partake in the usual banter you experience at the office, tend to crack jokes that fall flat. My advice: save it for the comedy club or at least when you are in person. Because guess what? If you aren't professional with the boss and your colleagues, the assumption is you're too casual and clueless with everyone—including the customers.

WHERE ARE YOU? STILL CAN'T HEAR YOU.

Of course, the many temptations are challenging. The most obvious scenario goes something like this: You've been sitting in your home office for hours. You have a taste for a grande macchiato, and there's a Starbucks with Wi-Fi and plenty of tables right down the block. They'll never know—or so you convince yourself.

You're on mute (how brilliant is that!), and when your boss asks you a question, you slyly (or so you think) unmute for a brief moment to speak. But I guarantee it, that's when the barista will start grinding beans, which sounds like a squadron of F-22s flying through the room. Then there's the gaggle of schoolkids in line. and music pounding in the background.

You cup your hand over the phone, slide under the table, slink off to the corner by the restrooms (nope, there's a speaker blaring music there, too).

Where are you? Still can't hear you. It's the litany of remote-worker disconnection.

It's going to happen occasionally. Your boss calls you while you're

in transit (but if it's during work hours, you'd better be going to or coming from an appointment). Or it's lunchtime. (I have a running joke with one of my colleagues who works remotely that every time I call him, he's crossing the street.) That can happen even if you never work virtually, but you just happen to be out when that call comes in.

Working remotely can give you a false sense of invisibility—they won't know where you are. Trust me, they do. I can tell when the people I'm talking to are in stores, restaurants, and every mode of train, plane, and automobile imaginable. My daughter related how she once sat next to a woman who was getting a mani-pedi and could be overheard telling someone she "had just stepped out of a client meeting, but had a moment to talk."

THE PHONE-CALL HIERARCHY

I can't say this strongly enough: never forget where you are when you take a call. There is a hierarchy at work here. The basic rule of thumb is, the higher up the person you're talking to, the more urgent it is that you be in a quiet, professional environment with no background noise. Here are a few guidelines:

IMPROMPTU CONVERSATION WITH YOUR TEAM.
If you aren't at your desk, engage in the conversation, answer the urgent matters, and if there is more to discuss, arrange to speak when you're back at your desk (or in a quieter place) within a few minutes.

IMPROMPTU CALL WITH YOUR BOSS.
Decide based on where you are (and how quickly you can get someplace quiet) whether to pick up immediately or call back in five minutes.

REGULARLY SCHEDULED CALL.
In the quietest and most professional environment possible. Don't eat or engage in any other activity. Make your coffee before the call. Shut the door if you aren't alone or if the kids or pets are in the habit of bursting in unannounced.

CALLS WITH THE BOSS AND HIGHER-UPS.
Quiet, professional, no muting allowed. Period.

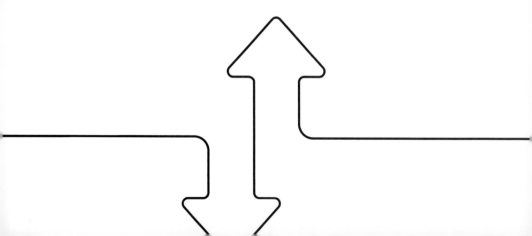

MUTE IS
NOT MAGIC

People think the mute button has magical powers. Simply push it, and suddenly everyone thinks you're in a glass-enclosed high-rise office. They'll never know you're in the grocery store ("cleanup on aisle four") because you forgot to buy arugula and you hate going to the store after work. But muted conversations come across as weirdly staccato. It's like bad audiotape editing, and it goes like this:

> **Boss:** Where do we stand with the *XYZ* project?
>
> **In-office team member:** We've done the specs, gotten quotes for the cost, and we're just double-checking the timing.
>
> **You, working remotely:** [Unmute] I agree! [Mute] Talked to B.J. [Mute] All set. [Mute]
>
> **Boss:** Where are you?
>
> **You:** [Unmute] [Burst of fake laughter] [Mute] Right here. [Mute] At my desk. [Muted silence, but not before that giveaway blast of the latest Starbucks playlist at full volume.]

Trust me, people know. Not only can it be difficult for you to manage (*Oh rats! I'm not on mute!*), but it's distracting for everyone else. They can't help but wonder: Where are you and what are you hiding?

If you can only take that call when you're in an airport, then say so. If it's noisy and you have to mute yourself, let everyone know you're doing it as a courtesy, but stay connected. And for the record, that's the exception, not the norm.

MUTED—OR CHECKED OUT?

Don't be that person who feels the mute button works as an excused absence, like a doctor's note to get you out of that 12-person conference call that no one wants to be on. We all know these people— once they hit mute, it's permission to disengage, and no one ever hears from them again.

This one really gets me. Someone on the group call asks "John" or "Mary" a question. Then—silence. "John/Mary, you there?" More silence. So the group moves on. A couple of discussion points later, John/Mary blurts out breathlessly, "I'm here—I was just on mute." What a joke! They were not present. They stepped away, got distracted, or became busy with emails. Whatever the cause, it surely wasn't the forgotten mute button.

And then there are people who think they're muted but aren't. The dog is barking up a storm. You can hear typing on a keyboard. And you can hear that little chime every time an email hits their inbox. Listening to this symphony of barking and pinging, I can't help but wish, *Please go on mute!*

STAYING CONNECTED

Where does this leave you? In the end, I hope you're a little less complacent about working away from the office. Respect the challenge that it is. If you do, there is power in knowing and preparing for all that can go wrong, and even more power in being prepared in a way that few others are. It takes a special sense of awareness to be a virtual worker, but the reward of kissing off four-hour commutes and seeing your kids actually come home from school is worth all those hours of learning how to stage a professional Skype face.

Success in working virtually comes from staying connected—and not just digitally.

No matter how flexible your arrangement—even if you get to work from a cabin in the most remote area of Montana—you're still part of a team. You need to be **SEEN:** *showing* you can be productive, *engaging* with the team, *entering* the office strategically, and *never* forgetting where you are for those all-important team calls.

Working in a WeWork World

More and more these days, freelancers, consultants, and others in the gig economy are flocking to coworking and shared office spaces like WeWork. Companies too are embracing this new reality of the "work anywhere, anytime" career nomad. At Korn Ferry, we're using coworking spaces (as well as virtual work arrangements) to give people more flexibility in how and where they work.

For advice on what to do before and after you take the leap, we reached out to WeWorkers and other shared-space veterans—designers, artists, writers, salespeople, marketing professionals, consultants, and others—both inside and outside Korn Ferry. Here's a compilation of what they had to say:

BEFORE YOU COMMIT

What's your motivation?

The first step is knowing why you want to pursue a coworking environment. Will you be there every day to replicate the feeling of being in an office? Or are you craving social interaction, and working from home just doesn't cut it? Are you getting a break from a long commute a few days a week? Do you need an office environment to conduct business and meetings? Or is your employer offering a shared space as an option for greater flexibility? Know your why before you pick your where.

CONTINUED

Social or lone wolf?

Do you feed off the energy of others working around you? Virtual working environments can be a real melting pot of ideas, energy, and enriching conversations. Or are you more of a lone wolf who wants little interaction while you're working? Your preference for how you like to work will be the most important deciding factor in the type of shared space you choose.

Know the choices.

There is a wide variety of venues and vibes among shared spaces. Some replicate a traditional office environment with desks and cubicles, as well as glass-enclosed spaces for privacy. Others have an open floor plan with a more social atmosphere, including after-hours activities and full-service bars that make it feel more like a club. And there are specialized spaces, such as for writers and other creatives. On the other end of the spectrum, there are sublets within large offices, complete with conference rooms, reception areas, someone to answer the phone, and a fancy address. It's all about finding the atmospheres that fit your taste, style of working, and personality.

Music or the sound of silence?

Before you commit, get a feeling for the sound level where you'll be working. Is there background music? Is it enjoyable? Tolerable? Distracting? If you need quiet or near-silence when you work, then you'll need either more private space or really good noise-cancelling headphones.

What's your space?

Shared work environments offer a variety of arrangements, from "hot desks" available during the day to dedicated desks and glass-enclosed cubicles. Other options include communal tables, with people to your right and left, or camping out on a sofa with your laptop. What's your preferred space—flexible and casual or more structured?

Who's going to pay?

The size and type of space and the services included vary widely in cost. There may be plans for full-time and part-time use. Know your budget and who is going to pay for the space—you or your employer.

Know the rules.

Every space has different rules for such things as noise level, whether you can take phone calls in communal areas, and bringing in food and beverages from the outside. Make sure those rules work for the way you work!

Respect the boundaries.

The tighter the space, the more critical this becomes. If you're at a work-table with eight other people, don't spread out. Make room for others to do their work undisturbed. Also be mindful of the layout: "hot desks" are meant to be shared, but dedicated desks are off-limits to anyone except their assigned user. Clean up after yourself.

Use your emotional intelligence.

Be mindful of others around you and their nonverbal cues. That person sitting five feet away wearing headphones and staring at the computer screen doesn't want to make small talk. In fact, view headphones as a signal that people don't want to be disturbed.

Socialize and network in common areas.

Communal areas, where people gather for coffee or to have a meal or snack, are venues for socializing and networking. While taking a break in these areas, you'll have more opportunities to introduce yourself and strike up a conversation.

Check out special events.

Networking events, guest speakers, musical performances, yoga medita-tions, wine tastings—most spaces have events and activities that bring members together and offer a chance to experience the social side of the community. If this is valuable to you, events can allow you to meet and mingle with others who have similar leisure interests, beyond sharing a coworking space.

Consider your wardrobe.

We're not telling you what to wear, but you'll probably find the style is very casual. One shared-space worker, who spent more than four decades in a very conservative office environment, told us he's had to shed his cuff links and ties in his new digs. But he doesn't seem to mind, joking that he's going to start wearing skinny jeans with holes in them—and maybe get a tattoo.

YOUR 5 TAKEAWAYS

FOR SUCCESSFULLY WORKING VIRTUALLY

Show that you can be productive anywhere.

Engage with your boss and team with frequent check-ins by email, text, or phone—whatever mode of communication the group prefers.

Enter the office strategically, such as for those monthly meetings, when the big boss is in town, or for brainstorming sessions.

Never forget where you are when you have important calls. The mute button is not a cure-all.

Demonstrating what you do is only half of the equation. Be connected so others can see who you are.

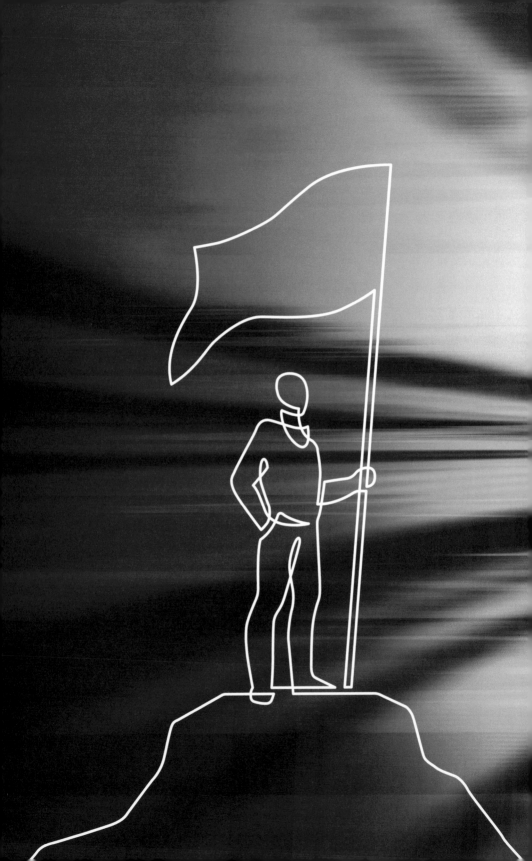

Chapter Eight

MANAGING FOR THE FIRST TIME:

Things Just Got Real

There are many exciting and important moments throughout your career. The raise you didn't expect (but deserved!) comes through. You're given a new title, put in charge of an important project, or transferred to a high-profile division. While all these can be confidence boosters and do advance your career, none come close to the importance of being made a manager for the first time. *You. People. In charge. The boss.* It's a whole different world.

Interestingly, this shift can happen at almost any stage of a career. Some people fresh out of college get tapped to run a small team. Others go years as individual contributors, preferring or doing quite well in the trenches. But no matter how or when a first-time management gig starts, let me be very clear. This is a big moment—a huge chance to succeed or, conversely, fall flat on your face.

For better or for worse, companies generally give higher salaries and fancy titles to those who lead—not those who are led. So unless you work for yourself and only yourself, you're not going to get ahead unless you embrace and excel as a manager. Even though managing is fairly commonplace, and it's a role that's been around forever, it's hard to imagine anything more challenging. Just look at some of the tasks the role can require:

OVERSEE A STRANGER. Suppose you moved into a new neighborhood and a friendly couple knocked on your door with a cake. "Hi, we wanted to welcome you to our neighborhood. Now, would you please start ordering us around, controlling a huge portion of our lives for eight hours a day, five days a week?" That's essentially what it's like to be brought in as a new manager.

ORDER FRIENDS AROUND. The reward for being the best on the team is often to be put in charge of the very colleagues you work with. You're managing the people you lunched with and bonded with; now you have to motivate, inspire, and monitor them. And deep down, you're probably praying that they've forgotten all the complaining you've done about the boss and how you were all treated—now that you are the boss and have to make those same demands on people.

BE RESPONSIBLE FOR YOUR DIRECT REPORTS—IN *EVERY* WAY. First-time managers rarely fathom this, but your career is entirely in the hands of others. That isn't all bad; much of this chapter will discuss motivation and how to trigger it. But for the moment, consider how much responsibility you have now for the little details: approving vacation time, deciding if someone can work from home, reviewing expense reports. Plus, you now must be the educator and official sheriff for all things corporate, because the firm expects you to pass down and enforce all of its

Q I've just been promoted to a manager position for the first time. What's the most important thing I should be aware of?

A Top of the list for a first-time manager: your words and actions matter. There should be no gap between what you say and what you do.

policies, rules, and goals. Each of your direct reports depends on you to know all and explain all. *Can I take a late-night Uber from the office? Are jeans OK on casual Friday? What did the CEO's announcement really mean?* "I don't know" is not an acceptable response and neither is a wrong one.

DEAL WITH THE TEAM YOU GET. Even a sixth grader learns how to pick a good mix of people to play tag, but first-time managers rarely get to pick their team. Instead, they're thrown into a group with a wide range of skill sets, personalities, and motivations and are asked to succeed in running that team—which probably includes some low performers. Good luck with that!

ENJOY THE HOT SEAT. It's no exaggeration to say that from day one, every word you say, every action you take, every facial expression you make will become an echo chamber, reverberating over and over for all to see, hear, and interpret. It's also no exaggeration to point out that any

slipup—an inadvertent slight to a colleague, a casual knock on your CEO, an inappropriate joke—can be the death of you. Emails are particularly a minefield, since they're so easily forwarded. Indeed, no manager can forget the power of the forwarded email!

BEWARE THE POWER OF THE FORWARD BUTTON. From the day you become a first-time manager, you'll need to consider carefully what you put in writing, even to other managers who someday may be working for you. Think long now. Have you ever written anything like:

"I need to you to pitch in here and pick up for your colleague Sam. He can be a little slow."

"Agreed. The CEO should tell people this in person."

"This conference call is doing wonders for my insomnia. Zzzzz."

"Everyone thought I was in the office, but I was on the golf course—Skyping calls."

"If he isn't being helpful, just nod a lot and pretend you're listening to the advice."

HOW BEING
IN CHARGE
REALLY WORKS

Now that I've properly scared you, I'll also tell you the flip side of managing: few things in life can be as rewarding, because you can create a future for others and push them far beyond what they dreamed they could do. In doing so, you're helping get them ready to assume positions and earn salaries that can be truly life-changing for them and their families.

A friend of mine once showed me a scrapbook her father kept from the days before electronic transmission ruled, of all the letters he received from the grateful people who worked for him. Many of those notes dated decades back and expressed heartful praise and gratitude. As a manager today, you're less likely to get such letters— people don't work for the same bosses as long. But the truly successful manager isn't looking for gratitude as much as success among his team. After all, this is exactly what will make him or her successful.

The trick is really understanding how being in charge works. It may be tempting to pull the authority card—*I'm the boss and you have to listen to me!*—except that isn't how it works. It should be clear by now: while managing others may make you feel as if you're the one in control, the irony is you actually have less control. Up to this point, your success rested on your shoulders. Now you have to rely on others—it's on their shoulders. If your team isn't successful, you won't be.

It starts with your mindset. Rather than "control, power, authority," think "teaching, accountability, responsibility." This means putting others first.

Yet human nature being what it is, that may be more of a challenge than you'd like to admit. Think back to when you had your first taste of authority. Maybe it was when you were much younger. You were the school crossing guard and got to wear that flashy white vest. Maybe you were a hall monitor, homeroom captain, or the person who picked teams on the schoolyard. You liked being in charge, but it went to your head. In short, you acted like a jerk and nobody wanted to follow you.

The blunt truth is people don't leave companies as much as they leave bosses. As a first-time manager in your first real leadership role, you must appreciate the simple fact that without followership there is no leadership.

THINK "TEACHER": ACCOUNTABLE, RESPONSIBLE

One of the biggest challenges, and a potential stumbling block, is understanding that what got you here (i.e., being technically proficient in your job) won't help you now that you're a first-time manager. You need to master new skills to develop and motivate others. That's why you need to think of yourself as a teacher—you are accountable and responsible for others.

In the military, for example, leaders put the safety and well-being of others before themselves. I've met a number of West Point leaders who led during periods of conflict, and many have voluntarily told me, "I've never lost a soldier." This reveals a deep mindset of humility and accountability, rather than hubris and bravado.

As a manager, you won't face such life-or-death situations. But you must make sure you don't lose anyone. Ask yourself: What does each person on my team need to grow, learn, and advance?

As you shift to a teacher mindset, keep in mind the 70-20-10 rule: 70 percent of what people learn is from experiences on the job; 20 percent is learned from other people—especially their boss. That means that you, as a manager, have a direct impact on 90 percent of how people on your team learn and grow. The remaining 10 percent comes from formal training—and you probably have to approve that, too! With a teacher mindset, you make others' career development your priority.

Ken Blanchard, one of the best-known experts on leadership, tells a story about his days as a young college professor, when he made it a habit to give out a copy of the final exam on the first day. The students were thrilled, but his fellow faculty members were not. Often, Ken had to explain himself. His job, as he saw it, was to teach the students the content they needed to be successful. Making sure they learned was far more important than administering a final exam.

Take the same approach as a manager: empower and enable others to learn so they can become even more successful.

The Winningest Football Coach's Playbook

Coach John McKissick of Summerville High School in Summerville, South Carolina, who had the most wins (621 to be exact) of any football coach at any level, used to put it this way: "It's players who win games, but coaches who lose them." As a first-time manager, you need to take this advice to heart. Adopt the mindset of a teacher rather than an authoritarian in order to develop others, earn their trust, and inspire followership.

A poignant example of followership was walking the halls with Coach McKissick. "Hey, coach," a young man called out excitedly to him. "Next year! I can't wait— I'm playing for you!"

That's the kind of followership a manager or leader at any level wants to foster.

THE TRAPS OF BEING A FIRST-TIME MANAGER

As a first-time manager, you face a lot of new responsibilities: creating alignment, establishing goals, monitoring individual and team progress, and inspiring others to achieve even more than they thought possible. And you may feel unprepared for the role, especially if you are still in the early stage of your career. It's a common problem. The *Wall Street Journal* reported on the University of Pennsylvania's Wharton School offering an undergraduate (yes, undergraduate, not graduate) class on "How to Be the Boss." The aim is to help prepare new bosses who are still in their 20s, who may find their companies aren't adequately training them.

Equally important to know is what *not* to do. Here are some common traps to avoid:

IT'S LEADERSHIP, NOT FRIENDSHIP. This one can be tough. You want to be liked, so you try to be everyone's friend. But there are tough calls and decisions to make around everything from time off to assignments, raises to promotions. If you're fair and transparent, you'll be respected—and that's more important for you as a manager than being liked.

PEOPLE WILL TELL YOU WHAT THEY THINK YOU WANT TO HEAR. As a first-time manager, one of the troubling realities you will encounter is the tendency of most people to tell you what they think you want to hear. This will only get worse the higher up in the organization you go. The fact is, people who may have been your friends when you were colleagues may suddenly become guarded or hesitant around you. They'll filter what they say, with a bias toward good news instead of telling you the whole truth. From your first day as a manager, you need to make it safe for others to tell you the truth. Listen to what you *don't* want to hear, including when someone gives you feedback on what's going wrong or not working out. This is exactly the feedback you need, without sugarcoating.

NO DISCONNECT BETWEEN YOUR TALK AND YOUR WALK. Mirror the behaviors you want to see in others. Actions really do speak louder than words. Treat people with respect, value their input and opinions, and do your best to make informed decisions.

SLEEPING SENTRIES GET YOU KILLED. Now that your success depends on others, you need to make sure every person on the team is contributing. Evaluate your team; if someone can't get the job done, you need to address it. People issues don't age well. You need to make tough decisions, including whether to fire someone who can't pull his or her weight.

DON'T GET SUCKED INTO THE DRAMA. As a first-time manager, you'll have more emails than you ever imagined. Not only are you hearing from the higher-ups about what needs to be accomplished, you are also on the receiving end of every email that a team member escalates up the chain. Plus, you'll be cced on everything. You can easily get overwhelmed by requests for days off, questions about random company policies, complaints about coworkers, and so forth. And if that isn't enough, people will expect immediate answers from you. You'll soon find out just how high-maintenance people can be when you're the one who can approve that day off or that work-from-home arrangement. Yes, this is the nitty-gritty of managing, but do your best to stay above the fray. You can't get sucked into the drama.

NO GOSSIPING. Talking about other people is never a good idea, but it may have been tolerable when you were one of the team. But as the boss, you can't—period. It's unprofessional, and you'll lose your team's trust. If you gossip, people will assume that you're also talking about them when they're not around.

YOU CAN'T PLAY FAVORITES. A casual lunch with a team member isn't so casual anymore. You can't give the impression of spending more time with one person versus the others.

KNOW WHO YOU'LL NEVER WIN OVER. As a first-time manager, you'll probably have someone on your team who wanted your job. But you were hired for a reason—your boss saw you possessed the capabilities for developing, motivating, and directing the team. If the other person can get on board with you—great. If not, don't go out of your way to win him or her over, because, as harsh as it may sound, it probably won't work. The person will either get over it or leave.

ENABLING OTHERS TO BELIEVE

Being a good manager or leader is all about inspiring others to believe—in themselves, in the organization, in what's possible—then translating that belief into reality. You need to forget all the lauded, impressive qualities that helped you get here, and shift your focus to others.

Easy to intellectualize, but hard to actualize. Fortunately, there is a framework for you to follow—now, as a first-time manager, and throughout your management and leadership career.

12 MUST-HAVES FOR THE FIRST-TIME MANAGER

1 Purpose: This encompasses the what and the why of the organization. Purpose fosters alignment across organizations in which thousands or even tens of thousands of people are making countless decisions and taking innumerable actions every day. With purpose, people are more likely to act in concert with the mission and objectives of the organization. Without purpose, individuals and teams can easily go off track.

2 Strategy: This is the game plan to realize the purpose—the how and, more subtly, the when. Strategy is purposeful and definitive, yet also flexible and adaptable, responding to an ever-changing environment. It starts with the results of today and lays out the path to the future.

3 People: The truly essential element is the people who will embrace the purpose and execute the strategy. Rather than simply being a collection of stars, a team must be a mosaic of talents and abilities working together, complementing each other, and carrying the organization forward.

4 Measure: What's working and what isn't? Measuring and monitoring how much progress is being

made will carry you forward into action. Direct feedback from your team and customers will help you identify where the organization is successful and where it is missing the mark. Results matter most.

5 Empower: Delegate opportunities, not just tasks. A goal of leadership is not to tell people what to do, but rather to tell them what to think about. Enable and equip others—then get out of their way.

6 Reward: It's more than compensation—it's a celebration. Acknowledge the incremental steps, not just final results. When people feel appreciated, they will do more, because at the heart of it, people want to know that they belong to something that is bigger than themselves. They want to be seen, valued, and loved.

7 Anticipate: Create a vision of the future that others cannot yet see. This isn't just imagination. Anticipation is always grounded in the reality of today, by identifying the current trends and triggers and then extrapolating their meaning for the present and future. As you look beyond the next turn, you expect and predict, but you don't guess.

8 Navigate: This is course-correcting in real time. Navigating takes clarity to see emerging opportunities, honesty to admit mistakes, and courage to make real-time decisions toward a new way forward. When you navigate, strategy isn't a once-a-year exercise—it's thoughtful and ongoing.

9 Communicate: Don't just transmit information—connect emotionally with others and inspire. Communication is critical for building alignment and executing strategy. It is the leader's "information highway," and it flows in both directions. Communication is important in good times and imperative in challenging ones.

10 Listen: Listening is not just hearing the words; it's also paying attention to nonverbal cues to see how a person feels and what he or she might be thinking. Listening is your monitoring system to discover what's really going on—and it takes diligent practice.

11 Learn: Be insatiably curious and engage in a lifelong passion for learning. The more you learn, the more you will improve—and you'll also bring the organization along with you.

12 Lead: You need to be all in, all the time. As a manager, you can't have a "gray day," because your mood will be interpreted by everyone around you. (If the boss is worried, should we be worried?) Model the attitude and behaviors you want to see in others.

Giving
Feedback

One of the biggest challenges for a first-time manager is giving feedback. (In fact, at times feedback can be harder to give than it is to get.)

Here's a common scenario: You delegate tasks to your team but notice that the work isn't being done the way you'd do it. You're so frustrated, you regret handing off the project!

Focus on the long term. Even more important than the task at hand is having the opportunity to develop your team by providing real-time feedback on a project or task that's in progress.

Give feedback starting with the positive, add your criticism in the middle, and end on a high note. Set expectations for follow-up and check-ins.

This is an opportunity to learn and grow— for your team and for you.

MOTIVATING
OTHERS TO SUCCEED

To be a good manager, you need to motivate others to succeed. Ideally, people are driven by their own sense of purpose, and they are aligned with the overarching purpose (the what and the why) of the organization. This is the utmost in intrinsic motivation.

What else drives behavior? Yes, the extrinsic motivation of earning a reward does make an impact, as does the opportunity to be recognized. Some people are motivated by the challenge of the work itself. And I've never known anyone who didn't appreciate a sincere thank you; when people feel seen and valued, they'll be motivated to do more.

Understanding motivation is a science. As I explained in Chapter One, "Taking Control," one of our firm's early thought leaders, David McClelland, did extensive research into human behavior and motivation and identified three key internal drivers: achievement, the desire for mastery at the individual level; affiliation, meaning to establish and maintain relationships and belong to a group; and power, which in this context means having an impact or influence. As McClelland's work illustrated, these motivations generate needs, which in turn lead to aspirations. And those aspirations drive behaviors.

As you understand the motivations among your team members—achievement, affiliation, or power—you can help channel each person's self-interest into shared interest. This is what I call going from "me" to "we." Interestingly, I observed this in action with my own children a few years ago. It was our last day of vacation at a beautiful beachside condo. As we scrambled to pack—my wife and I and our five children—

YOU CAN HELP CHANNEL EACH PERSON'S SELF-INTEREST INTO SHARED INTEREST.

somebody knocked over a fruit smoothie the color and consistency of pink lava. Naturally, it landed on a white rug. Cleanup quickly devolved into chaos as someone grabbed bath towels (white, of course) to sop up the mess, and someone else had the bright idea of squirting shampoo on the rug, then dousing it with water.

As the mess got worse, everybody retreated to his or her own self-interest: my wife to her fear that we'd miss the flight; me to my concern that we were going lose the exorbitant rental deposit because of a five-dollar smoothie; and each of the kids to denials that he or she was responsible.

Except Emily. She stayed with the task, even though it wasn't her drink or her accident. When I asked her why she was working so hard, she shrugged and smiled. "I'm having fun." Her positive attitude quickly shifted her siblings from "me" to "we." The mess got cleaned up and the disaster was averted (except when the blow-dryer Emily used to get the water out of the carpet singed it like a blowtorch).

Emily didn't know it, but she demonstrated what a first-time manager should do—moving everyone from self-interest to shared interest. We even made our flight.

One way to facilitate the shift from "me" to "we" is by making the desired behaviors contagious among your team—acting as a kind of positive form of peer pressure. Think about what happens in a typical suburban neighborhood when the first few houses put up Christmas lights—suddenly, everybody else does it too. Or a few households start planting flower gardens and landscaping; the next thing you know, the entire neighborhood is in bloom. The same thing can happen within teams as first a few and then more people begin to adopt the desired behaviors that reinforce shared interest.

Another tool you have at your disposal to encourage and lead your team forward is goal-setting, which is a big part of management. Goals establish expectations, create a broader understanding of what success looks like, and deliver greater value to the organization. Savvy managers make goal-setting a transparent and motivating process that lifts the efforts of individuals and the entire team.

One more thing: most people like to have goals. They like to measure themselves against a standard and be measured by people they respect and who make a difference to them in life and at work. Goals need to be realistic but also stretching, so that you can do more than you initially thought. Goals can make things fairer as an equitable way to measure one person against another. People like it even better when they participate in a fair goal-setting process; it's even more motivating to them to have a hand in setting their own stretch goals.

Unlocking the Potential of Your Team

Think of three accomplishments you're proud of, then ask yourself: How motivated were you to accomplish each?

That exercise can help you realize the importance of motivation to unlock the potential of your team. If you can figure out what motivates others, their accomplishments and yours will be greater. Some managers believe that others should be automatically motivated, thinking motivation comes standard with the person. Some managers believe that everyone should be as motivated as they are about the job and the organization. That's seldom the case. People are different in the way they become motivated and sustain that motivation.

COMMITTED TO YOUR TEAM

As a first-time manager, your success will come from your commitment to your team. You must continually meet the needs of those who follow you. Think "teacher"—making sure others are developed and equipped to succeed. And think "shepherd"—occasionally in front, sometimes beside, but mostly behind. Then, wherever you're going, others will willingly go with you.

YOUR **5** TAKEAWAYS

FOR BECOMING A GREAT FIRST-TIME MANAGER

Be self-aware as you lead by your actions, not just your words. Your team will watch what you do even more than they will listen to what you say. Model the behaviors you want to see in others.

Leadership requires followership. Your success as a manager is solely dependent on the success of others. If your team doesn't perform, you won't progress.

Think "teacher," not authoritarian. Own the job of manager and the responsibility that comes with it.

Know what motivates your team—purpose, mission, and the intrinsic drivers that shift self-interest to shared interest.

Sleeping sentries get you killed. Make the hard "people decisions" faster rather than slower.

Chapter Nine

PRESENTING WITHOUT PANIC:

Dodging Death by PowerPoint

Spiders...heights...small enclosed spaces...Everybody has fears. For most, it's public speaking—as it is for Panicked Paul, who starts pacing back and forth as if he's playing ping-pong, dripping with sweat. Or Scared Scarlett, who turns her back to the audience and speaks to the screen while clicking through her innumerable PowerPoint slides. Monotone Marty, Trembling Terry ... You've probably heard and seen them all. And,

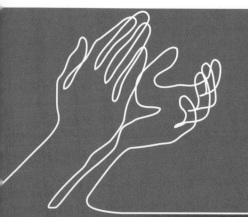

Q I've been asked to make a presentation. I'm nervous! How do I avoid bombing?

A Think **LIKE** (which should be easy, since that's what you're aiming for).

L → Lose the PowerPoint.
Too many slides are a crutch—and 37 PowerPoint slides never won anybody's heart. People want to hear you.

I → Identify who your audience is.
Find out what they want to know and how you can connect with them. This presentation is all about them—not you!

K → Know your message.
Three main points, three subpoints. List the bullet points. Have the right mix of stories to engage and information to share.

E → Embrace the practice.
Most of us have to practice—a lot. Video record yourself to see and hear what you say and how you say it. The more you speak, the better you'll do. So practice, prepare, and practice some more.

truth be told, maybe they describe you: shirt soaked under your arms, gritting your teeth through technology breakdowns, and clicking your pen like you're the Little Drummer Boy. The worst case I ever saw was someone who became so panicked he just left the podium.

What happened? It's true: fear of public speaking ranks right up there with fear of death. (Comedian Jerry Seinfeld said it best: the person in the casket might be better off than the one giving the eulogy.) When one thing goes wrong—and, believe me, it will go wrong (microphone, projector, sound system)—you may begin to unravel.

But there's a deeper reason for this agitation. Everybody is motivated by the same basic desire to be liked and accepted. We never really get out of sixth grade! When you're speaking to one or a few people, you probably feel more at ease. If it's a group of peers, they know you and vice versa. But with a large audience, it's so easy to lose sight of things—even with the exact same presentation. Your anxiety rises disproportionately as the number of people increases. It's the fear of failure!

You're totally focused on what your audience thinks about you—not what they want or need to hear. And that's where it all comes apart. You become overwhelmed by thoughts of whether they like you. Your fears and insecurities ramp up until you're drowning in a cesspool of anxiety.

One solution to panic is preparation—this is no time to wing it. There are a gifted few who can make a performance in front of thousands feel as intimate and meaningful as a one-on-one conversation. It's effortless—as if they were born doing this. Believe me, they weren't. Professional speakers and those who give keynotes for a living have coaches. They study clips of their performances like a football quarterback reviewing the reels from previous games. If you have a smartphone, you can do the same. Practice, practice, and then, when you're on, all that preparation will take over and you'll do just fine.

You'll be able to give a coherent, confident six-minute update at the next team meeting, even if your boss's boss slips into the room just before you're up—and you start to feel that telltale trickle of sweat.

L → LOSE
THE POWERPOINT

PowerPoint presentation: if ever there were a misnomer, that would be the one. A PowerPoint is not a presentation. It doesn't speak—it can't present. The presentation is done by a person—the slides are only visuals.

But I'd bet that the majority of people reading this disagree. They can't bear to part with their precious PowerPoint decks. They're enamored of their fancy slides and slick video clips. Whether they're giving a speech or providing an update at a meeting, they'll spend hours on their PowerPoint files. They'll think nothing of displaying 38 slides covered with text in small print, as if the entire purpose of the presentation were to read what's on the screen. If that were the case, then you'd just print out the slides and skip the presentation!

Over the past 10 years or so, presentation prep has become increasingly more focused on constructing good PowerPoint slides and far less on the words. That's the default for most people. *Have to make a presentation? Better start with PowerPoint … *Wrong!

People want to see and hear you. That's the secret to LIKE—you're the messenger and the message, not that pie chart with a tangle of lines

Death by PowerPoint

✔ Lose the PowerPoint crutch. Don't expect the visuals to do your job for you.

✔ Use half as many slides (or even fewer!) as you think you need. PowerPoint should illustrate—not make—the point.

✔ Don't expect people to read what's on the screen.

✔ If you must give detailed information, send a meeting brief well in advance.

✔ Stop using slides cluttered with too much information—and in a font that is just too small.

and labels, columns of incomprehensible numbers, or a cluster of words you have to squint to see as if it's an eye test.

Now, there are times when you need to use PowerPoint to assist you in making a presentation. Maybe you have to provide a certain overview of information. Or you have a compelling photograph or graphic that will really enhance the experience for the audience. Or you're introducing a new concept or product.

Just keep it simple! Use as few slides as possible. Make sure each is appealing to the eye, with enough blank space that the information and graphics stand out.

If you have to share information that's in-depth and detailed, then send out briefing material several days in advance—not that morning or the day before. Give people enough time to read and digest the information so they're listening to you, not reading the presentation. Even then, your slide deck should be supplemental to what you have to say. You want to educate your audience quickly, bringing everyone up to speed on the latest information so that you can move quickly to the Q&A.

Bottom Line Up Front

Make every slide count, especially when you have to give detailed background information. One effective way of doing this is giving the **bottom line up front**.

In this format, the title of each slide is the concluding point. For example:

SLIDE 1: Strong Market Opportunity

SLIDE 2: Opportunity Limited to the Northeast

SLIDE 3: Our NE Market Share Expanding

One slide to the next, the titles tell the story in sequential order. The details are found in the body of the slide. If people do nothing but read the slide titles, they'll be well prepared to listen to your presentation and engage in a meaningful discussion.

I → IDENTIFY YOUR AUDIENCE

When you're asked to make a presentation, the first questions to consider are: Who am I speaking to? And what do they want to know? After all, this presentation is all about them—and that's the first step to making that all-important connection with your audience. The more relevant your message, the more the audience will give you their time and attention. And believe me, your audience will take only a few seconds to decide whether to tune in or tune out. It's oddly similar to what happens in a job interview. (See "What a Job Interview Can Teach You About Making a Presentation" on opposite page.) If you make a connection with the other person from the opening moments of that interaction, you're far more likely to have a successful interview. If the connection isn't there, then it's over even before it's begun.

Unfortunately, too many presenters—and even the experienced ones—get this wrong. They put all their emphasis on themselves and what they want to say. This is a huge mistake. Don't think you have a captive audience. Even if they can't get up and leave, they'll tune you out. Your listeners' attention must be earned, not taken for granted.

As you outline your speech, ask yourself:

- **What does the audience—individually and collectively— need and want to hear?**
- **What experience should they be having?**
- **What will make it relevant and meaningful for them?**
- **How can you connect with them?**

WHAT A JOB INTERVIEW CAN TEACH YOU ABOUT MAKING A PRESENTATION

I f you've been asked to make a presentation—at a team meeting, in front of the entire department, or maybe (gulp!) with senior leaders in the room—you may feel as if you've wandered into totally unfamiliar territory. Relax! These are all very similar experiences—you probably just don't think of it that way. While they may seem dissimilar, that's only on the surface (one or two people in a conference room vs. a dozen in a meeting room vs. several hundred in an auditorium). The ground rules still apply:

The Seven-Second Rule

It's a statistic you've probably heard quoted frequently: it takes people only seven seconds to make a judgment about others. In a job interview, the interviewer will make several snap judgments about you—including your likability, your trustworthiness, how assertive or passive you seem, and how well you would fit in with others on the team. **The same seven seconds apply to your presentation. Each audience member is going to make a snap decision about whether your message is worth his or her time and attention.**

Know Your Audience

Before your job interview, you'd ideally look up all the information you could about the hiring manager and other people you were scheduled to meet. You'd check out their LinkedIn profiles, find out as much as you could about their backgrounds, and look for common ground so you could make a connection. **The same due diligence applies when making a presentation.** You should know as much about the audience so you can deliver as relevant a message as possible. Are they technically proficient? No need to overexplain. Are they from different areas of the company? Forge common understanding and align to overarching goals.

CONTINUED

Be Memorable

To be in a successful job interview, you'd tell a story of a challenge you faced or how you were part of a team that launched something new, fixed something broken, or found new and different ways of doing things. These stories and details make you memorable to the interviewer. **These are the same things that will make you memorable to an audience.** It isn't just about facts and figures—stories and examples are what make the information meaningful and memorable.

K → KNOW YOUR MESSAGE

Once you identify your audience, it's far more straightforward to know your message. You aren't just downloading everything in your head; rather, you're targeting a message that your audience needs and wants.

As obvious as this may seem, some people get it wrong—like Wandering Wally, who never met a tangent he didn't like, or Um-Uh Ursula, who puts more useless space between her words than a crossword puzzle. (*Today, uh, I want to talk, um, about the database project that, uh, we're working on …*)

Know what you're talking about. By that I mean you have to know your subject matter. If you're winging it, your audience will know—and quickly. The first hint is that you are talking in circles.

Make an outline: three main points. Any more than that and people will feel overloaded. Within those main points, you can make about three supporting points. Think sound bites—you're conveying your message 30 or 40 seconds at a time. Write it all down, use bullets, and organize your material so the flow is logical, one point leading to the next.

Don't get lost in the tangents—and, please, don't decide to go deep into the background so you can show how much you know. (They know you know, that's why you're the one presenting.) The more organized you are with what you're going to say, the more impact you'll make. Stick to your time allotted and leave room for questions. Going over is not only rude, it shows you are unfocused and unprepared.

Depending on the kind of presentation or speech you're giving (hint: this won't apply as much if you're giving a quick update), you can capture attention and create emotional buy-in by telling a story. Ideally, that story begins the moment you stand up to address your audience. Avoid the typical (read: boring) opening of "I'm So-and-So, and today I'm going to cover three things." Remember, you only have a few seconds at the opening to grab your audience's attention. In that blink of time, they're trying to decide whether to tune in or tune out.

A story can tune them in—a short anecdote that illustrates the point you want to make. The more personal and compelling, the better. Then the audience will be far more likely to settle in and listen to you.

Storytelling can be a very effective tool in giving a speech or a longer presentation. (If you're just giving an update at a team meeting, your story should be a quick anecdote that takes about 20 seconds to tell.)

Here are a few tips for effective storytelling:

- **Illustrate with an example. Describe what happened in a situation, event, or experience.**
- **Draw from a past experience and identify what you learned.**
- **Use metaphors when appropriate, especially when conveying the emotional impact of what was or is involved.**
- **Balance inspiration with facts—say or show what you value in words or actions (within the parameters of your style, of course).**

Making a Solid Presentation

Make a list; check it twice. What are the main points you want to make? Whether you're hosting a conference call, making a presentation at a group meeting, or giving a speech, you need to start with the main points you want to convey. Frame your main ideas as bullet points (usually about three to five—any more than that can feel like information overload).

Keep visuals to a minimum. I said it before, but it's worth repeating here. If you must use visuals, use them only to illustrate or amplify the points that you're verbalizing. Less is more. What you say and how you say it will make a far bigger impact.

Say your piece, then stop talking. If asked to give an update, do just that, and in the time allowed. And make sure you explain in a way that makes it engaging and understandable. Don't try to impress people with your in-depth knowledge or technical expertise.

Be the answer person. Anticipate questions. Do your homework and have the relevant facts and figures at hand. If you don't know something, it's perfectly acceptable to say, "I know whom to ask, so I'll get right back to you on that."

E → EMBRACE THE PRACTICE

Listen, I've given hundreds of speeches, but I never, ever wing it. You need to practice, practice, practice. How effective are you in what you say and how you say it? Watch your body language. Do you face the audience, or are you turning your back to them so you can read those PowerPoint slides you were supposed to lose? Is your posture relaxed and confident? Or do you look like you're in a police lineup? How are your hand gestures—open and inviting? Or are you chopping wood with your hand? You want to be part of your message, not distract from it.

Are you able to convey your key points and subpoints in the most concise, meaningful, and engaging way possible? Do you stay within the allotted time, with room for questions?

The more you practice, the more ingrained the presentation will become. Then when you get up in front of the room or at the podium, the practice will take over. Display a little nervousness and you'll be forgiven. But if you're unprepared, you'll be either forgotten or dismissed as wasting time.

So the next time you feel that fear of public speaking, you can push the **PANIC** button:

P REPARE—a lot and more than you think you need to. Record video and play it back to hear and see yourself in action.

A UTHENTIC. Be who you are. You're the one who was asked to give this presentation! If you try to be something you're not, the audience will think "phony" and tune you out!

N EVER let them see you sweat. Remember Murphy's Law: if something can go wrong, it will. Make sure you have your handouts and notes before a presentation. If you're giving a speech, go to the room ahead of time. Check the technology—microphones, sound system, etc. And always have a Plan B for what can, and probably will, go wrong.

I DENTIFY your audience. As discussed, you need to know who they are and what they need to know. If you're presenting in front of people you don't know, mingle ahead of time. Shake a few hands and introduce yourself. They'll already be warmed up to you before you speak.

C ONNECT with each person. Speak to each person. (There are tricks to this, such as moving your gaze across the room slowly and stopping at intervals—see "Delivering with Confidence" on opposite page.) Make sure your message resonates.

WHAT DO YOU DO IF YOU BOMB THE PRESENTATION?

You're presenting in front of a major client and everything goes wrong—technology glitches, you can't find your notes, and you've never felt more unprepared in your life. Your boss has to step in to do damage control. You bombed—so what do you do?

1. Admit the mistake. Far more important than what happened is how you handle it. By owning the mistake instead of trying to get past it as quickly as possible, you'll decrease your chance of failing that way again.

2. Apologize sincerely. Don't shrug it off. You need to make a sincere apology—not 10,000 excuses for why it happened.

3. Move forward. You need an explicit action plan to show you've learned from the mistake and are working to improve your presentation skills. If necessary, ask for training or coaching to improve your ability.

DELIVERING WITH CONFIDENCE

POSTURE

→ Get in seated "ready position": sit tall, feet flat on the floor, hands open on the table.

→ Get in standing "ready position": balance weight slightly forward.

→ Stand tall, relax knees, relax arms at sides.

PAUSING

→ Pause between thoughts for one to three seconds.

→ Breathe during your pauses to relax and energize your voice.

→ Listen for "nonwords" and pause instead.

→ Shorten sentences to avoid rambling.

PACING

→ Avoid the extremes—moving back and forth like a metronome or standing still like a statue.

→ Move fluidly, then stop and deliver a few points at a time: center, left, center, right.

PODIUM

→ Lose it, if you can. Have nothing between you and your audience.

EYE COMMUNICATION

→ Look at each person for three to six seconds (for a phrase or a sentence).

→ Include everyone.

→ Be random, avoid patterns.

→ Talk only to eyes.

NATURAL ANIMATION

→ Gesture freely within the given space, matching the ideas expressed.

→ Vary your gestures—one or two handed.

→ When not gesturing, relax arms and hands—no clasping or fidgeting.

→ Smile when appropriate, even on the phone. Relax your face and match the expression to the message.

→ Vary vocal inflection and pace to conversational tone and to avoid monotone or uptalk.

THE EVERYDAY PRESENTATION

Maybe you don't give speeches or presentations regularly. That still doesn't get you off the hook. The reality is, you are presenting all the time—the next team meeting, conference call, or conversation in the hallway. Each is a presentation of your ideas and yourself. Master these small presentations, because they're the real make-or-break moments in your career.

One of the most common everyday presentations is the conference call. While this seems mundane (who doesn't have conference calls all the time?), you can't underestimate their importance—or their annoyance. Face it: half of conference calls are a waste of time. The purpose is unclear—is it to share information, gather input, make decisions? There are too many people on the line. They run over, somebody has a bad connection, and there's annoying background noise. People are coming on and dropping off the call unannounced. There are those who say nothing and others who won't shut up. The mute button is permission to disengage.

How to Be a Great Everyday Presenter

- It's not only what you say but how you say it—body language, facial expression, and nonverbal cues.
- Focus on your listeners—first, last, and always.
- Know what you're talking about.
- Listen more than you talk—you want dialogue, not pontification.
- Keep to the point and respect people's time.

You can half-listen and do something else (catch up on emails, fold laundry at home, play with the dog). Except you can almost guarantee that the minute you're in your email and only half-listening to the call, your boss will ask you a question. Once again, this is a matter of being prepared. Know your content and be ready.

If you're the call organizer, have an agenda and share it with others. If you want certain people to give an update, ask them in advance with parameters of what you're expecting. A one-minute status report? A five-minute overview? Is

IF YOU'RE THE ORGANIZER, HAVE AN AGENDA AND SHARE IT WITH OTHERS.

this a call-in that's voice only, or will it also include visuals? Make sure people have all the information they need so they can fully participate.

More often, you're one of several participants on someone else's call. Know why you're on the line and what's expected of you. If your boss suddenly asks you for an update or to answer a question, be prepared to respond. And you can never be sure of who is listening—your boss's boss or people whose roles and influence aren't clear to you. Show up and be present!

At the same time, you need to be savvy. Most of the time, the agenda is unclear—or, more likely, there's no agenda. Usually these calls are freeform and chaotic. In this weird ecosystem, you can't wait to be called on. Be agile and go with the flow. Speak up when it matters. Don't try to take over a call that's not yours, but be a meaningful contributor. No matter how disorganized and chaotic others are, you can be the one who's prepared, knows the message, and stays on target and on topic. That's the way to rise above the rest.

One way to approach everyday presenting—on a conference call, in the next team meeting—is to think of yourself as the host. This is especially effective with unscripted events such as a team discussion. And it really applies to networking events or a meet-and-greet at a conference.

Too bad no one ever told that to Bombastic Bart, who likes to hold court every chance he gets. At every industry event, you can find Bart at some table (usually near the free shrimp appetizers), bending the ear of two or three people who haven't found a polite way to extricate themselves.

Or Pontificating Polly, whose favorite expression seems to be, "And another thing …" Whenever she's got the floor, she'll go on—and on—thinking that this captive audience is hanging on her every word. Polly doesn't notice the glazed and pained expressions from people who instantly tune her out but are too polite to leave.

Needless to say, they aren't the role models you want to follow. When you're a good host, you bring people together into meaningful dialogue. It's like you're giving a dinner party and you want to make sure everyone feels welcome and involved. Ask engaging questions. Seek out others' viewpoints. You'll make a lasting impression as someone who really knows how to bring them together and foster discussion.

And that's the secret to success for making a presentation, whether you're speaking to two people or two thousand.

YOUR 5 TAKEAWAYS

FOR MAKING A SUCCESSFUL PRESENTATION

Lose the PowerPoint. Your slides aren't doing the presentation, you are.

Know your audience: who they are, what they want to know, and how you can make your message meaningful to them.

Make a connection. The first seven seconds matter.

Be organized. Have three main points and a few subpoints. Know your material. No tangents allowed.

Practice, record, review, and practice some more. And then do it again.

Chapter Ten

"LET'S HAVE A MEETING":

Why They're All Meaningless

You can always tell when a company has become too bureaucratic. The rote response to almost everything is "let's have a meeting." It's such an epidemic that people now mistake the meeting for the action. How about solving the problem today?

It's no secret that most people don't like meetings: too long, too boring, too frequent, too many people, and too often not accomplishing much of anything. People check out—on mute during conference calls, doing email, catching up on the sports scores.

Think about it—how many times have you stopped by someone's desk who's obviously on a call, but the person assures you "it's OK, we can talk." The call is on mute and he's having a conversation with you, instead of paying attention to what's being said on the line. If that isn't a clear indication of too many unimportant meetings, I don't know what is. Author and leadership expert Patrick Lencioni calls it "death by meeting."

It isn't just a case of multitasking—it's escapism. People obviously want to be somewhere else besides that meeting, so they are only nominally present. I was at a company recently where people on opposite sides of the conference table were obviously texting each other. One would

Q I attend so many meetings—most of them unproductive. I can't get any real work done. What should I do?

A Meetings these days are the solution to everything. If there's a problem, you have a meeting. If there's a new opportunity, you have a meeting. Schedules get so crammed, you can't get anything meaningful done. Every meeting must pass a test: What's the purpose? That will quickly eliminate a lot of them. And the meetings that remain will become much more impactful.

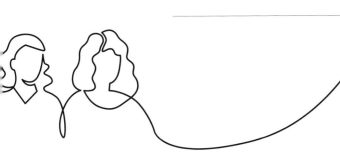

look down and type furiously; a faint buzz would go off, and the other person would start typing. I doubted they were using their texts as a sort of teleprompter about what to say next. The exchange went on way too long for that. So why were they in that meeting? Why not just go out to the hallway and talk?

Learning when and why to call a meeting is very important as you advance in your career. Bosses aren't the only ones who arrange meetings—team leaders do, too. Even if you're tasked with a project, you may request to meet with your colleagues. But don't mistake having a meeting as a sign of your authority or proof that you're a good manager or project lead. Do that, and people will groan every time they get yet another meeting invitation by email and start scrambling for excuses to get out of it.

The problem is so pervasive, everyone can relate. Someone posted a particularly insightful comment on my LinkedIn page recently in response to a column I wrote about unproductive meetings: "Too often the lack of preparation and clarity of action destroy morale and create a culture of resentment toward meetings. At a certain point in the organizational hierarchy, many people believe that talking is the same as work, and meetings are products in themselves." Too true.

I can guarantee that almost everyone has regularly scheduled calls they dread. You know those meetings—when that reminder pops up, you literally wince. Regularly scheduled calls are the worst. At first there are a dozen people on the call. After a while, the four "optional" people don't show up. Then some of the "mandatory" people start dialing in late and leaving early (or they go mute and disappear). Suddenly, only a few die-hards remain: the organizer and the two or three people who can't afford to skip. These are sure signs of dead, unproductive calls with no purpose or meaning.

So forget those weekly status meetings—they just aren't realistic in today's global business environment, in which things move quickly. If you're the one scheduling those calls and meetings, be honest: Are people enthused to participate? Is it a good use of their time? If not, find a better way to gather updates.

And if you're a participant, don't be passive-aggressive by muting your line or texting under the table thinking that no one knows (they do). Have the courage to speak up and ask whether this call or meeting is even necessary.

Meeting by Walking (and Calling) Around

Sometimes the most effective course is to skip the meeting altogether and go straight to action. Management expert Tom Peters coined the term "management by walking around," which, as the name implies, involves managers who wander at random to talk to people. I do my own updated version of that—in person and virtually. I call it "meeting by walking (and calling) around."

Rather than scheduling a meeting to get an update or delve more deeply into a situation, I'll have an impromptu discussion with someone. I'll stop by an office in person or pick up the phone and call. I've been known to surprise people who are a few levels below the C-suite to draw out their input. I'll also take a walk with my cell and call people to get the pulse of what's going on. Ditto grabbing someone for lunch at a local deli.

No formal agenda. No script. Just talk—that's what makes this so productive.

THE REAL PROBLEM WITH MEETINGS

The problem with meetings, experts say, is timing—as if better scheduling solves everything. There is an entire body of research dedicated to finding the best time to meet. The worst time, they say, is Monday morning. Some argue that people are their most productive on Monday morning as they get up to speed on the workweek. Having a meeting would only break that momentum and distract them from what needs to be done (the "urgent" things that require their immediate attention—more on that later). Plus, people may take Mondays off for the occasional three-day weekend, making it likely that there will be some no-shows for that Monday-morning meeting.

The optimal time for a meeting, behavioral scientists say, is 2:30 p.m. on Tuesdays. Some combination of after-lunch biorhythms and a sense of "not too early, not too late" supposedly makes this a magic time for meetings. (Others say that's also a good time for going to the Department of Motor Vehicles—go figure.)

But all those scientists and behavioral experts neglect to address one important thing: In a global company, participants on that conference call may spread over three continents—it's going to be morning somewhere. So with all due respect to the scientists, I don't believe the real problem with meetings is the *when*. It's the *what*—as in, what's the purpose of the meeting? To explain, think **MEET:**

M → Make it purposeful

E → Elicit collective genius

E → Embrace constructive conflict

T → Take action

By following these four steps, you'll make meetings more meaning-ful and worth people's time.

M → MAKE IT PURPOSEFUL

Before I call any meeting, I start with the end in mind. This is the "M" in **MEET**—making it purposeful! What, specifically, are we trying to accomplish, and how will a meeting (as opposed to a phone call, a quick in-person conversation, an email, or even a text) move things along?

That's why I always take the BLUF approach: bottom line up front. It focuses on what needs to be done, who is going to do it, and by when. Know what you want to get out of the meeting. Is it just informational, or are you making decisions? What action plan will result? If you leave any meeting without answers to those questions, you've just wasted your time!

NIX THE BIG FORMAL AGENDA

If you've got 12 topics on your agenda with two or three sub-bullets for each point, people will be exhausted just read-ing it! They'll be watching the clock, try-ing to figure out how long this meeting is really going to take. It's better to have two or three things you want to discuss. More items than that will cramp the discus-sion and stifle creativity.

FOUR TYPES OF MEETINGS

One way to make your meetings more purposeful is to know what kind of meeting you're having. I put meetings into four categories:

INFORMATIONAL: This is to get an update on what's going on, but it still needs to be actionable. We aren't just talking about what's been done, we're going to set expectations for what needs to happen moving forward.

DECISION-TAKING: This is all about what action we are going to take. By definition, this type of meeting must involve a smaller group than other meetings. Once you have more than three to five people, it's difficult to make decisions. And at the end of this meeting, a decision will result.

DISCOVERY: This type of meeting is for discussing problems and potential solutions. Once again, it isn't just talk for talk's sake—the focus is on action.

BRAINSTORMING: Here it's all blue sky with no bad ideas. For these creative sessions, I suggest going off-site to get people out of their comfort zones. This departure from routines and habits, I've found, helps stir people's thinking to really envision the new and different.

The 45-Minute Rule

A half hour is too short when you spend the first five to seven minutes with small talk—the weather, sports, family, vacations ... Meanwhile, an hour-long meeting tends to drag on (I subscribe to the theory that people will take all the time you give them). Forty-five minutes is usually the sweet spot. You're looking for solutions that are 80 percent right and 100 percent executable versus the other way around. With time management (and no long agenda, remember?), you'll get to solutions and actions more quickly and efficiently.

MATERIALS TO SHARE? THREE MINUTES IS NOT "IN ADVANCE"

No matter which type of meeting you're having, if there are materials to be reviewed, they must be distributed in advance—at least a day or two beforehand. Three minutes is not "in advance," which is what happened to me recently. I kid you not: at 9:27 a.m., a PowerPoint file hit my email inbox for a 9:30 meeting. I couldn't believe it when the person who called the meeting said, "You've received the materials," as if we were all speed-readers. (That's maddening for sure, but let's not go there—see Chapter Nine, "Presenting Without Panic.") Because no one had sufficient time to review the materials, we spent most of the meeting flipping through the PowerPoint slides together like we were in a second-grade reading class and it was Johnny's turn to read aloud. What a waste of time!

Meetings are so much more productive when people get the materials in advance with the expectation that they'll read it all beforehand. With this background and context, the meeting discussion goes much deeper— and that's really important for an informational session that goes beyond reviewing what's already occurred to setting a course for the next steps.

SELF-REFLECTION: A MEETING WITH YOURSELF

With the pace of business accelerating these days and technology keeping us plugged in 24-7, we can't negate one of the most important meetings a person can have—alone time for self-reflection. It's a great habit to get into early in your career and to develop as you advance to becoming a team leader, manager, and beyond. Find some time each day—often early morning or in the evening—to contemplate your day. What's going well? What could be improved? What do you need to do next?

My self-reflection time is very early in the morning. I devote an hour or two without interruptions to reading the news from a variety of international sources, catching up and responding to emails, and thinking. For me, this is the most productive way to start my day.

E → ELICIT COLLECTIVE GENIUS

Now we move to the first "E" in **MEET**—eliciting collective genius. You never know where the best ideas will come from. That's why, with the exception of decision-taking meetings, you'll want to include as many people as possible (within reason, of course). To get things rolling, I often start these sessions by going around the table (in-person or virtually) and asking each person, "What do you think?" (I'll usually close in the same way.) This not only jump-starts the discussion, it also sends a clear message that everyone's ideas and perspectives are welcome, and everyone is expected to contribute. I want open and honest discussion (and even some constructive conflict, as we'll discuss next).

Here's what I *don't* want: a performance. This is really a pet peeve of mine. When people meet with senior leaders it often becomes a performance—scripted and rehearsed. There's the meeting before the meeting, and the pre-meeting before that. And after the meeting, there's the call to discuss how it went. That's a lot of time invested before we even dig into the discussion.

URGENT VS. IMPORTANT

If you've got a crisis on your hands, then what you're facing is both urgent *and* important. But those scenarios, thankfully, are few and far between. More likely, you'll have urgent issues and you'll have important ones. You need to know the difference. *Urgent* should be dealt with ASAP by the right people with the right resources. *Important* is another matter. Strategic and longer term in nature, important issues can be the subject of meetings to update information, discover problems and solutions, and determine an action plan. Never get so bogged down in urgent matters that you don't have time for the important ones.

I get it. People want to be prepared and make sure they're delivering meaningful information, especially when meeting with senior leaders. But when it feels like I'm sitting in the audience at a play, it's just too much. There's no spontaneity. Everything that everyone says has been planned out and rehearsed in advance.

Even more troubling, though—and one of the biggest frustrations for any CEO—is that people tend to say what they think you want to hear. Often, it takes a long time to establish any kind of trust and candor. In the meantime, it can be like pulling teeth to get at what's really going on or to chip through the sugarcoating to uncover the problem.

The irony, though, is that almost every meeting I participate in has to do with problems. It goes with the function. Problems escalate, and by the time they reach the CEO, it's probably controversial or involves competing interests. Or it may be that nobody will risk making a decision. But if that discussion is scripted or if people are holding back on what they say, it isn't productive.

To increase the chances of convening collective genius, try these:

✔ **INVITE A DIVERSE TEAM.** Research shows that the more diverse the group, the more options they typically identify. Groups that are more alike tend to come to decisions too quickly and often choose the most likely scenario.

✔ **ENCOURAGE CONSTRUCTIVE** conflict by establishing ground rules.

✔ **HAS THE TEAM GENERATED** at least two alternatives that make the most sense? Research also illustrates that teams considering at least two alternatives made decisions they consider successful about two-thirds of the time—versus only half the time for teams considering only one alternative.

✔ **WHAT ARE THE PROS AND CONS?** On the upside, what can be gained if you take a certain action? On the downside, what are the risks if you act (or don't act)?

Breakfast, Lunch, and Dinner

What's the real benefit to having a discussion over a meal—breakfast, lunch, or dinner? Too often, I've found, people don't think this through. Maybe it's their organizational culture to "eat in" frequently—so why not grab coffee and a bagel before that early-morning meeting or work late and order pizza? If that works for your team in your environment, then great.

But what about when someone considers having a meeting at a restaurant in order to share a meal together? This can work, but there are limitations.

BREAKFAST. Let me say this up front: I'm not a big fan of breakfast meetings. The early hour combined with the need to get to the office immediately afterward can distract people and make breakfast meetings unproductive.

DINNER. I've found these are usually far more social occasions than business meetings. That certainly isn't a bad thing. Dinner meetings can be very effective for getting to know other people (clients, strategic partners, and other important contacts). But the combination of a multicourse meal after a long day isn't conducive to having an in-depth business discussion.

LUNCH. This is the best meal to share while having a productive discussion. It may be the informality of the meal or the fact that it occurs during the workday. Whatever the reason, lunch meetings can be an extension of an in-office discussion, but with a change of venue that helps stir ideas.

E → EMBRACE
CONSTRUCTIVE
CONFLICT

The second "E" in **MEET** is where things get really interesting. It's all about embracing constructive conflict. That's challenging for a lot of people. People don't like conflict. If you're honest, you may be one of those people—you want things to be harmonious. (Maybe you were even raised in a family where conflict was seen as a bad thing.)

The problem with no conflict at all is that people end up nodding and yessing you to death—and all the while, they're thinking the opposite. But they don't say what they think, which means important and even crucial information is withheld, all out of some well-intentioned but ultimately misguided desire to make everybody else happy.

The solution is constructive conflict. I've addressed this in Chapter Five on coworkers, but it bears repeating here: conflict is not to be avoided. It takes some degree of conflict for the best ideas to emerge. When you get smart people together to discuss a problem or an opportunity, it's only natural that there is some conflict. If you're the meeting facilitator, you need to be comfortable with conflict around you—and with conflict directed at you.

The conflict never gets personal, of course, and there's no reason for anyone to raise his or her voice. The conflict is about the issue at hand. Even colleagues who have the utmost respect for each other can have intense conflicts at times because they view things differently.

So the next time someone speaks up and says, "I completely disagree," don't shut it down or try to gloss over it. Let all sides be heard, and chances are you'll have more confidence in whatever solution you decide is the best of all possibilities.

T → TAKE ACTION

Now we come to the "T" in MEET—the culmination of the previous three steps: take action. Just as you set expectations for what you want to accomplish at the beginning (the BLUF approach), you need to bring the meeting to a close with an action plan. If you began with the end in mind, you should come full circle: with the game plan of what comes next.

Before they walk out that door or disconnect from the conference call, everyone must know what's expected of them—and by when. Purpose is what sets the stage for a meaningful meeting, and action is what differentiates it from being merely a group conversation. With purpose and action, even long meetings are engaging.

YOUR 5 TAKEAWAYS

FOR MEETINGS THAT MATTER

Less is more. Is calling that next meeting absolutely necessary?

Begin any meeting with the end in mind: What's the purpose? What's the intended outcome?

Collective genius can only come from open and candid discussion, not a scripted performance.

Constructive conflict enables productive disagreement to occur freely. It takes conflict for the best ideas, most effective solutions, and different thinking to be explored.

Close with action—make sure everyone knows what's expected and by when.

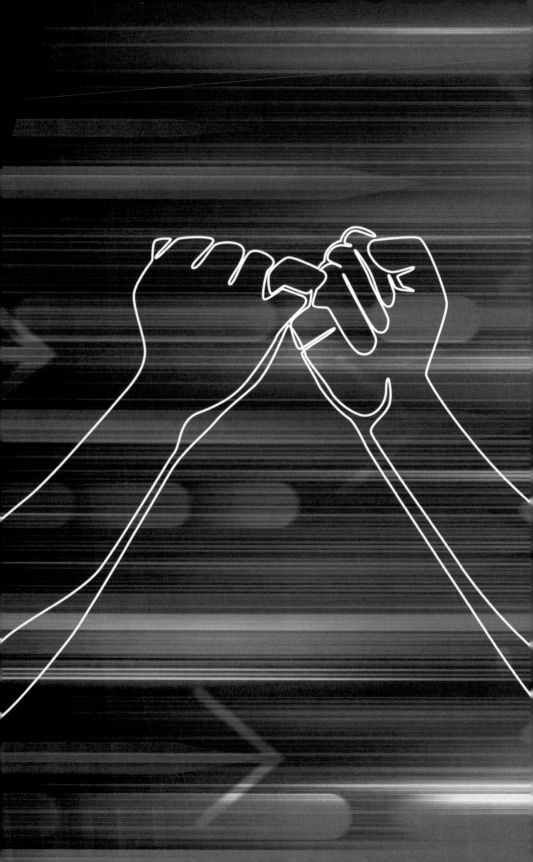

Chapter Eleven

NETWORKING WITHIN:
Find Your Champion

Extroverts think they're pros at it. Introverts dread it. Most people end up somewhere in the middle. "It" is networking. Some people think it's as easy as working a room and chatting up everyone they see. They'll dive into a networking event like a hungry seal in a school of fish. Or they approach it like a 1950s door-to-door salesman trying to sell vacuum cleaners to everyone he meets. This is not networking; it's stalking.

NETWORKING POORLY IS WORSE THAN NOT NETWORKING AT ALL.

The fact is, networking mystifies people—and the reason, I've decided, is that they dread it so much. People feel awkward asking for help, and the idea of reaching out to someone has all the appeal of cold-calling to sell those handy slice-and-dice-it knives you see on late-night infomercials. This raises an even bigger point: networking poorly is worse than not networking at all.

You have to know how to do it—and not just to get your next job. Networking is also crucial for advancing in your *current* job. Within your company, you're looking to connect with people who can open doors and teach you how things get done in the organization. Every organization has an informal network of "influencers" (see Chapter Six, "Building Political Capital") who work largely behind the scenes. These are the people you definitely need in your internal network.

Just remember: networking is all about building relationships. That's why I call it a "contact sport."

THE POINT OF CONTACT

If you haven't thought about the care and nurturing of your network until now, you're behind the curve. Connecting with people for the sole purpose of asking for their help will put off many of them—especially if they don't know you well. And that applies to your internal and external networks.

Q How can I increase my visibility within my company?

A First, perform. Build relationships by leading with what you can do for others. You can increase your visibility from there by leveraging your internal network.

Many years ago, when I was working for a large consulting firm, I received a frantic call from someone I knew vaguely. "Sarah" and I had crossed paths a few times, but we certainly weren't close colleagues. But to hear her on the phone, you'd think we worked closely together every day. The reason Sarah kept pushing this point was she was undergoing a 360-degree review and needed to come up with names of people who could speak to her accomplishments—by the next morning!

"I'd like to help," I told her, "but I'm not sure what I can say."

She insisted: "We worked together on the *XYZ* project, remember?"

"No, that wasn't me," I told her. "*XYZ* is not my account."

"Well, you can think of *something* to say—do you want me to write it for you?"

The harder she pressed, the more I had to wonder: Just how far down the list was I, and how many people had she already contacted?

Clearly, Sarah hadn't built and maintained her internal network. Maybe she didn't think it was a valuable exercise until she really needed something. That's never a winning strategy.

You know what that feels like. You haven't seen or heard from someone in years, then suddenly that person reaches out to you because he or she wants something—trying to get promoted or wanting an introduction to someone. You probably won't be that inclined to help.

The same thing can happen when you're networking externally. Reaching out to someone you haven't had any contact with for years, just because you suddenly need help, is another big turnoff. Here's what happened to me: I hadn't seen or heard from "Joe" in more than a dozen years. While we worked in the same industry, our paths seldom crossed, other than in the most tangential way at industry events. And we were not friends outside of work. What I did know about Joe was from the financial news: several years before, he had pleaded guilty to insider trading and spent a few months in jail. Never during that time did he reach out to me. Never in that time did anyone we knew in common reach out to me. He was a distant memory and a familiar name in a newspaper article about an unfortunate incident.

So imagine my surprise when more than a decade after our last contact, Joe emailed me, requesting we "get together for lunch." He needed a job and was hoping I could give him some advice and introduce him to some of our recruiters. Really? My reaction had nothing to do with the fact that Joe spent time in prison for insider trading. From what I read, he took full responsibility for what happened. Rather, it was because his first contact with me after so many years—and given the fact that we weren't more than nodding acquaintances—was for help getting a job.

You may think I'm being harsh, but this is the reaction you're going to get from other people if you approach them from out of the blue. You may find someone who, for whatever reason, will help. But, quite frankly, that will be the exception and not the norm.

THE GOLDEN RULE:
IT'S NOT ABOUT YOU

Networking is about building relationships—and relationships aren't one-way streets. That's why the golden rule about networking is: *it's not about you!* Ideally, networking is grounded in what you can do for others. You can't take out what you haven't put in.

Right now, make a list of all the things you can do for people in your network. Even small things—if they are done sincerely and are genuinely meaningful to the other people (and those are two significant ifs)—can jump-start your networking. You're building goodwill with others for the day when you need help.

This is real networking, and it's all about what you can give to others. You may call that karma, paying it forward, or the reward for a job well done. I call it the fruits of networking: when you need their help, the people you've helped in the past will be more than happy to step up. Networking should be a natural behavior that comes from having a mindset of being genuinely interested in others and leading with your "give" before you seek to "get."

Check the Boxes

✔ NETWORKING REQUIRES AN OBJECTIVE.

Have a goal in mind so that your discussions with people have a purpose. When people in your network understand your goals, they'll gain clarity about where and how they can help you. Make sure your goals are focused on specific opportunities and positions—that promotion you want or that global assignment.

✔ MAKE A LIST.

Write down the names of everyone in your network, internal and external. This includes current and former colleagues, business contacts, members of professional organizations, even family, friends, and people you know socially. As you go through the list, think about the people you see and interact with regularly.

✔ MATCH CONTACTS AND OPPORTUNITIES.

As you categorize your contacts, think about the opportunities that are at the top of your wish list. Who in your network can help you? Who within your organization can make an introduction or connect you with someone? Who outside your organization can help you brainstorm or provide you with perspective from their own career journeys?

✔ BE RESPECTFUL OF OTHER PEOPLE'S TIME.

When you reach out to people in your network—whether to pick their brains or to request an introduction—you're asking them to do you a favor. Even if these contacts are close colleagues or friends, you can wear them out by constantly nagging for help. Chances are people will do what they can, but it's up to you to do the heavy lifting.

TAPPING YOUR INTERNAL NETWORK

The bigger your internal network, the more opportunities you'll have to grow. Having a broad network gives you access to more people so you can learn more about the company and what other departments do. Plus, as you establish connections with others, these contacts may hear of a job opportunity for you before it's posted.

My advice is to know as many people as possible. Be deliberate in seeking people out, but be smart about it, too. Here are a few tips:

LEAD WITH YOUR GIVE.

What information, insight, or assistance can you offer? Have you heard someone mention they needed help with a project or initiative? Company-sponsored charity events always need extra hands, and it's a great way to lead with your "give" and develop a reputation for going the extra mile.

REMEMBER YOUR ACT.

Whether you're networking, meeting with someone for the first time, or interacting in any other context, remember your ACT: be **authentic**, make a **connection**, and give others a **taste** of who you are. Getting your ACT together will make networking more meaningful as people will come to know the real you, not some persona you're trying to project to impress.

IDENTIFY WHO YOU WANT TO MEET AND WHY.

Instead of blasting out LinkedIn invitations to your colleagues, take a targeted approach to network in person. Know why you want to connect. Does this person have a lot of institutional knowledge? Does someone who recently joined the firm have expertise in a different sector of the industry? Or does the person work in part of the firm that you don't know anything about and you're eager to learn more?

KEEP YOUR FEET ON THE FLOOR—NOT IN YOUR MOUTH.

If you come on too strong, if you ask too much, if you try to "run into" senior people with stakeouts (in the kitchen, by the elevators, or near the restroom), you put yourself at

risk of coming across as awkward or acting strangely. You'll not only be embarrassed in the moment; you'll also end up cringing for the next six months—wanting to climb under your desk every time that person walks by. Be smart and professional in your approach.

IT'S CONNECTING—NOT VENTING. While you may bond over similarities like a mutual boss or alma mater, be mindful of what you share. You want to share enough to be connected, but not to the point of turning networking into griping.

DON'T EXPECT INSTANT MENTORING.
The people you connect with may be incredibly helpful. They may even encourage you to contact them whenever you have questions. But that doesn't mean you're now mentor and mentee. The mentoring relationship involves a commitment to be an ongoing sounding board and advisor—and that may very well be beyond what your contacts are offering.

MENTORS, SPONSORS, AND COACHES

Three specific types of people in your network can make a real difference in your advancement— mentors, sponsors, and coaches. Each role is distinct, which is why they should be different people. Let's take a look at each.

WORKING WITH A MENTOR

A **mentor is best thought of** as someone who takes you under his or her wing and helps you learn. In my own career, I purposefully chose to work for four bosses because they were such invaluable mentors. Having the opportunity to work for and learn from them determined the moves I made.

You may also have a mentor outside your company—for example, a former boss. Mentors outside your workplace may particularly help with getting a broader view of your industry and position. The best situation would be to have mentors both inside and outside your company for multiple perspectives.

While you should keep your eyes open for potential mentors, don't try too hard, as if you're trying to sell something. Don't be desperate! Rather, if you stand out among your peers, doing the things you want to achieve, then a potential mentor could very well seek you out.

Here are a few tips for making the most of a mentoring relationship:

EXPLORE YOUR OPTIONS.
You can access mentoring programs in many ways—for example, university alumni networks and online mentoring groups.
Plus, your employer may offer mentoring (nearly three-quarters of Fortune 500 companies offer some type of corporate mentorship programs).

LOOK FOR CONNECTIONS.
Don't just default to the easiest to access or the most obvious choice for a mentor. Instead, find a mentor who has been on a similar career path to yours or who shares a similar vision of success.

YOUR MENTOR IS NOT A MIRROR. While you should have some similarities with your mentor, that doesn't mean you need to be (or should be) mirror images of each other. In fact, some of the most productive mentor-mentee relationships can be more like sparring partners than best friends. Having a mentor who is unlike you also helps you access diverse viewpoints.

CHANGE THE EXPERIENCE.
Nontraditional mentoring can be enriching. For example, in "reverse mentoring," more mature workers engage with younger colleagues to upgrade their skills and keep pace with culture and the nature of work today. This can be very meaningful for both parties. The younger colleague also can learn from the broader perspective of the more experienced person.

SET EXPECTATIONS. Your mentor is a sounding board and advisor, not a personal job coach. Your mentor can help you understand and navigate office culture and politics and give some perspective from his or her own career journey. But don't expect this person to go to bat for you every time you want to get promoted.

EXPRESS RESPECT AND GRATITUDE. It's shocking how many mentors complain about this one: a mentee who cancels meetings and calls—or just doesn't show up! (In one extreme case I heard about, a mentee *never showed up* for any of the sessions scheduled with an assigned mentor.) Unreturned phone calls, violations of confidentiality, and feeling entitled to access the mentor's network are some of the more common derailers of the mentor-mentee relationship.

HAVING A SPONSOR

In addition to having a mentor, you may also attract the attention of a sponsor—someone higher up in the organization who can champion you. While a mentor advises you, a sponsor advocates and can help make the case for why you should be the one to get that assignment or promotion. One of my colleagues describes a sponsor as the person who mentions your name to others when you're not in the room. This is highly impactful—as research shows, people with sponsors are 23 percent more likely to move up in their careers than those without.

A COACH IN YOUR CORNER

Your coach is almost by definition someone outside the company. This is crucial because a coach brings an outsider's perspective with the objectivity that comes from knowledge across many companies and industries, and what others in similar situations have done. A coach is also someone you can be vulnerable with, admitting your fears and anxieties or venting frustrations (another reason for this person to be outside the company).

A coach will provide insight as to why you're unhappy in your current role or where you might be a better fit—for example, a large company over a small start-up. This will allow you to create specific goals and develop a plan with your coach on how to achieve them. Your personal coach is there to be a sounding board for your big ideas, empower your career growth, and help you make a change. (*KFAdvance.com* has more information on personal job coaching, what makes this relationship impactful, and how to find the best coach for your needs.)

GETTING VALIDATION

As you nurture your network, you are building relationships with people who will validate you, especially inside your company. These contacts are usually bosses and colleagues, as they know you from working and interacting with you. When they attest to your skills, your accomplishments, and your contributions as a team member or team leader, their words carry weight.

Maybe you know someone directly or have contact with "someone who knows someone." But when your path is indirect, you need to have someone vouch for you. And no one will vouch for you unless he or she knows you. When you find a person who is willing to put in a good word for you, you will be so much further ahead than if you try to go it alone.

Validation is not only good for you, it's also valuable to the company. Organizations today are trying to retain talent. While the reality of the career nomad isn't changing any time soon, getting people to stay four years instead of leaving after two (and turning those four years into eight) can be good for all involved.

To reduce the risk of a bad fit or advancing someone too soon, companies want to know if a person is ready for the challenge. That's where validation comes in. For instance, do you have a proven track record of quantifiable successes? This gives your next boss confidence that you are who you say you are, and that your career trajectory is real. Your organization wants to see that you can manage more people, generate more business, and take on more responsibilities. These are the signs of someone who is an outlier of achievement, with a winning track record.

FINDING AN OPPORTUNITY
WHERE THERE ISN'T ONE

One of the best possible outcomes of networking is getting a promotion or an assignment that didn't exist before you pursued it.

Maybe you want to work overseas, but there wasn't a position for you—that is, until you networked your way to meet the manager who runs the business in that part of the world, who then became convinced that you'd make a significant impact. Or maybe your willingness always to help others captured the attention of someone who decided you should be part of a team that's launching a key initiative. In both situations, people are willing to make a position for you. It does happen!

Companies want to hire and retain great talent. If you're motivated and you've got a great reputation and track record, it can all come together for you.

KEEPING SCORE:
GIVE VS. GET

As a final note—and this can't be emphasized too much—be mindful of how much you're "giving" and how much you're "getting." Your mentor or others in your network may not keep score, but *you* should! You don't want to deplete your goodwill or make others groan every time they get another request from you.

Here are 10 things you can do to build your network—internally and externally—by focusing on others first.

10 THINGS YOU CAN DO FOR YOUR NETWORK

(Which You Should Have Been Doing Already)

1 **Whom can you help?** Do you know someone else who is looking for a job? If so, reach out and offer to help, from brainstorming ideas to introducing him or her to someone you know.

2 **Which people in your network** have similar interests— professionally or personally—and would benefit from meeting? If you're all local, arrange to have coffee together. Or suggest that you connect them by email (with each party's permission).

3 **Whose child can you offer to help?** Maybe you've heard that the son or daughter of someone you know is thinking of applying to your alma mater, or is looking to enter a field similar to yours.

4 **Who has written a blog** that you can share within your social media network? Or can you leave a meaningful reply to the post? (This one is especially helpful if you are networking up the line with someone a few levels above you.)

5 **If you blog,** whom can you interview to gain his or her perspective on a topic? If your blog is well followed, this can help establish your contacts as subject-matter experts.

6 **What skill do you have** to offer someone? Are you good at social media? Can you help set up a simple website? Can you be a sounding board for someone who is launching a business or a new project?

7 **Whom should you congratulate?** Think of someone with a particular accomplishment or life event—a new job, an engagement or marriage, a new house.

8 **Can you recommend** a new restaurant, art gallery, or even a good book to someone in your network? Don't make your recommendation seem random. Let the person know why you thought of him or her.

9 **Whom can you invite** to a professional or cultural event? This is a great way to reconnect with former colleagues or other people you haven't seen in a while.

10 **Do you know someone** who is involved in a charity or community event and needs a volunteer? Giving your time, even for a few hours, is an excellent way to nurture your network and meet new people in a different context.

YOUR **5** TAKEAWAYS

FOR BUILDING YOUR INTERNAL NETWORK

Networking is a contact sport—it's all about building relationships. Lead with what you can give.

Think of it like hygiene—a daily habit.

Networking establishes connections with people who can offer validation when you need someone to put in a good word for you.

Seek out those who can positively guide you as a mentor, sponsor, or coach.

Even the best athletes have trainers—you should, too.

Part Three

TO
EARN MORE
YOU NEED
TO LEARN
MORE

It isn't like microwaving popcorn on high. Advancing your career takes time, effort, and insatiable curiosity. Learning agility is the number one predictor of success.

Chapter Twelve

TAPPING YOUR RIGHT BRAIN:

Don't Be a Know-It-All

It's a fatal flaw—thinking that you're so intelligent nothing else matters, not even how you treat others. One of the worst cases I've witnessed was a guy I worked with years ago. Yet in "Larry's" case, he really was the smartest guy in the room! He was brilliant and could discuss any subject—current events, politics, history, sports—with remarkable depth and insight. And when it came to job performance, Larry was amazing.

But Larry wielded his intelligence like a weapon. While I wouldn't be surprised if he had an IQ of 150, when it came to emotional intelligence, he was a 0. In other words, he was all "left brain"—he had skills that made him an amazing individual performer but was completely lacking in "right brain" people skills.

Now, before you dismiss this right-brain stuff as psychobabble or some kind of fancy way of saying you need to think creatively, hear me out. Skills that relate to your right brain include empathy, curiosity, adaptability, and the all-important people skills of influencing and motivating others. These are the skills that will distinguish you as you move through the six stages of your career, from individual contributor to manager and, one day, leader. (See Chapter One, "Taking Control.")

Larry, however, put no stock in his right brain. To say he was arrogant is an understatement. Since he was so much smarter than anyone else (as he'd be quick to tell you), Larry decided he didn't have to follow the rules that applied to everyone else. He routinely blew off meetings, and when he did show up, he talked over people, crushed anyone who disagreed with him, and was completely uninterested in anything anyone else had to say. After waltzing into a meeting late, Larry thought

Q I'm very good at what I do. I'm the best performer on the team—and smarter than everybody else, too. But I'm not getting promoted as fast as I think I should be. Why can't they see how valuable I am?

A Assuming you really are as smart and talented as you think you are, you're probably relying too much on your technical left-brain skills. That will take you only so far, however. You need to develop your right brain, which is all about connecting with, influencing, and motivating others. So, if you want to get ahead, especially in a position to lead and motivate others, you need a strong right brain.

nothing of flipping through a magazine while his colleagues made a presentation or discussed their latest win.

Larry was also tough to pin down on anything, from where he was to what he was doing. (Later, we discovered Larry was also a liar. Recently, I interviewed someone who probably knew him. When I inquired, the person replied, "Oh, of course I know him. The thing about Larry is he only lies when his lips are moving.") I can remember calling Larry on his cell, and he swore he was in one of our offices—except I could hear the road noise and the "ping-ping-ping" of the gas pump. (He loved driving his sports car.) His performance was so stellar, though, that people made excuses for him: "Oh, that's just Larry being Larry."

Over time, though, Larry's arrogance, intellectual superiority, and downright rudeness became highly toxic to the group. Let's just say he got voted off the island. Losing his performance was hard, but making the decision to ask him to leave was easy.

Most people have a little "Larryness" in them—only in their case, they overestimate how smart they are. They're so good at what they do (in their own minds, at least), they think it buys them a pass on everything else. To put it in the terms we use in this chapter, they're all about

Which Brain Are You?

LEFT-BRAINED
You're logical, analytical, and objective. Practical and pragmatic, you are more detail- and fact-oriented, and prefer to think in words and numbers.

RIGHT-BRAINED
A relationship builder, you collaborate and connect easily with others. You're intuitive, creative, and free thinking, and tend to think in terms of visuals.

You need both sides to advance in your career. But at some point, left-brain capabilities are assumed. As you advance, it's all about the right brain.

the left brain—their smarts and their technical skills (financial acumen, digital expertise, engineering background, etc.). But they are seriously lacking in the right-brain department.

It's a simple fact of life: what got you here won't get you there. If you really want to take control and advance in your career (and I'm not just talking about the next job), and especially if you want to become a leader one day, you'll need to develop another skill set. And the higher up you go, the more the right brain rules!

THE LEFT-BRAIN TRAP

It isn't that your left-brain skills don't matter. Both sides of your brain need to be developed so you can bring the best of yourself and your capabilities to everything you do. But even if you have deep and valuable technical expertise in a particular area—a left-brain

Becoming a Right-Brain Thinker

If you're naturally left-brained, you can develop right-brain capabilities. Here are a few suggestions:

BE OPEN TO NEW IDEAS AND APPROACHES. Instead of defaulting to the tried-and-true (which appeals to your pragmatic side), be open to trying varied approaches and new ideas.

EMBRACE AMBIGUITY. Practice coping with uncertainty and making decisions without having all the information beforehand.

TEST YOUR SOCIAL LEADERSHIP SKILLS. Motivate, influence, and connect more deeply with others. You might find you enjoy it—and even that you're good at it!

specialization, say, in engineering, laboratory medicine, finance, or the Internet of Things—you still need people skills to collaborate with others.

Let's put this in perspective. Early in your career, you were hired for your left-brain skills, which made you a good individual contributor who could get the job done. But once you reach a certain level, it's a given that you possess left-brain skills—they're the table stakes. To advance, you also need right-brain skills that are anchored in social leadership—influencing, motivating, and inspiring others.

I discovered this early in my career. With an accounting background, I went to work right out of college for what is now KPMG and spent many years in consulting. As I interacted with clients and colleagues, I quickly saw that while my left-brain skills in finance and accounting were a great foundation, I needed to hone my people skills. Years later, when I joined Korn Ferry and became an operating officer and then CFO, I still needed my left-brain skills, such as thinking strategically and managing risk. Then I became the CEO, and I needed to draw more than ever on my right-brain skills to motivate and inspire others, display optimism in the face of challenges, and be highly attuned to others. I even altered my communication style, shifting away from the PowerPoints I once relied on as CFO to focus much more on my tone, my attitude, and the energy I convey. It isn't only *what* I say but *how* I say it that matters.

> **TO ADVANCE, YOU ALSO NEED RIGHT-BRAIN SKILLS THAT ARE ANCHORED IN SOCIAL LEADERSHIP.**

Don't get caught in the left-brain trap of relying too much on your technical skills. From your first professional job out of college through your next positions and beyond, you should pursue jobs and assignments in which you can develop a full slate of holistic talents—drawing on the left brain and right brain.

THE RIGHT-BRAIN TEAM

Everybody today is trying to be a maxi-me in a mini world. They're trying to make their presence so much larger in a world that is increasingly smaller. You see this in the strangest ways—such as people taking selfies at their grandmother's wake (I kid you not). Despite this perception of the Insta-ME-gram world, it isn't really about you.

Success today is all about the team. And even if you are the epitome of the individual contributor—you spend hours by yourself in a research laboratory—you are still part of a team at some point. Everyone is, whether entry-level employee, mid-level manager, or senior leader. Companies spend an enormous amount of time, energy, money, and other resources on devising and building the best teams. Beyond that, there is a tremendous amount of research into what brings teams together. Needless to say, opinions vary broadly.

One of the most interesting studies focused on how personalities impact team effectiveness. It showed that the poorest-performing teams were 100 percent "pragmatic"—meaning they relied largely on their left-brain technical skills—and 0 percent focused on relationship building and other right-brain capabilities. In terms of team effectiveness, this was as bad as it gets.

To be fair, if you're left-brain oriented, you are valuable to your team. Pragmatism isn't a bad thing, either, although it can lead to linear thinking. But by developing your right brain you become a more effective team member—and that's a win-win. Plus, you'll be able to encourage partnership within your team, and between your team and others in the organization. Trust is established, which encourages growth and helps each person become his or her best self.

IT STARTS WITH SELF-AWARENESS

So how do you know what you need to do to become more right-brained? Like any skill development, you need to see yourself accurately—or, as I described it earlier, take a good look in the mirror. Its importance can't be overstated.

The difference between whether you advance in your career or get stuck (or worse, get fired) often comes down to self-awareness. In our research into why leaders derail, we've found that, all things being equal, self-awareness usually explains why some leaders succeed and others don't. Raising your self-awareness can keep you from derailing, as well.

What EI Means for You

HAVE YOU EVER:

- ✔ Ended up in conflict with someone?
- ✔ Felt overwhelmed with stress?
- ✔ Realized that a strong emotion is driving your reaction?
- ✔ Been surprised by someone's reaction to you?
- ✔ Felt that you just don't understand someone you work with?

No matter how bright you are, you can find yourself grappling with these issues because they require more than IQ—they demand emotional intelligence (EI).

Self-awareness is also at the heart of emotional intelligence (EI) and influences your ability to develop other competencies. A common problem among people who aren't self-aware is they overestimate their strengths and underestimate their weaknesses. (And underestimating your problem areas is just self-deception—see Chapter Two, "Uncovering Your Blind Spots.") You need accurate self-knowledge to clearly see your strengths and weaknesses, abilities and competencies, and passion and purpose, as well as the drivers that motivate you.

Engage in self-reflection by asking yourself probing questions: What old behaviors are holding you back? Where do you feel you need to improve? What do you do well and with confidence? Are you relying too much on your left-brain technical skills? Do you really possess the right-brain capabilities to influence and inspire others?

"YOU KNOW WHAT YOU ARE FEELING AND WHY."

And don't just take your own word for it—seek out informal feedback from others. What does your boss say about your work performance? What feedback are you getting from your mentor and coach? By combining feedback from others with the fruits of your self-reflection, you'll deepen your self-awareness.

But it doesn't stop there. Daniel Goleman, who is an expert in emotional intelligence, takes self-awareness a step further—adding emotion into the mix for *emotional self-awareness.*

When you're emotionally self-aware, you understand your own emotions and their effects on your performance. As Goleman explains, "You know what you are feeling and why—and how it helps or hurts what you are trying to do. You sense how others see you and so align your self-image with a larger reality. You have an accurate sense of your strengths and limitations, which gives you a realistic self-confidence."

Emotional self-awareness isn't something that you achieve once and then you're done with it, Goleman explains. Rather, you are constantly presented with opportunities to be self-aware, and in each moment you must choose. By drawing on your emotional intelligence and your self-awareness every time you can, you will make it an ingrained habit. You will be known for being emotionally self-aware—with strong right-brain capabilities.

Are You Emotionally Self-Aware?

Pay attention. That's the key to developing emotional self-awareness.

You know you're emotionally self-aware if:

✔ You are aware of your own feelings.

✔ You know why these feelings occur.

✔ You understand the implications of your emotions.

✔ You are aware of your strengths and limits.

✔ You are open to feedback.

You know you struggle with emotional self-awareness if:

✔ You easily get irritated with others.

✔ You treat people in an abrasive way without realizing the impact.

✔ You feel an imbalance between your work and personal or family life.

✔ You rarely seek feedback and find it hard to accept.

DEVELOPING EI
AND YOUR RIGHT BRAIN

Building and exercising your right-brain skills is a discipline like any other—you need new habits, practice, and feedback. Here are some ways you can develop and exercise your EI and other right-brain skills:

EMOTIONAL SELF-AWARENESS: Pay attention to situations that cause a physical reaction—a blush when you're embarrassed, your heart racing when you're excited or frightened, or sweaty palms when you're nervous or stressed. Become aware of what triggers these reactions and why. Notice the links between the physical signs, how you react to them, and the feelings that result. Consider keeping a log of your feelings and physical responses to help you become more emotionally self-aware.

EMOTIONAL SELF-CONTROL: Develop strategies to help you stay in control and keep your cool in difficult situations. A few simple steps can make a difference— counting to 10 really does help! Or step outside for a breath of fresh air, change rooms, get coffee or water. Think the opposite of the emotion that's being triggered; if you're feeling angry, think of something funny or silly, or sing a song in your head. These pauses can help you gain perspective and keep you from making a rash response.

A POSITIVE OUTLOOK:
See the good in others and in situations. Challenges are viewed as opportunities to grow, learn, do things differently, and achieve better outcomes. That doesn't mean you won't feel stressed or worried at times, but a positive outlook can help you navigate those feelings and stay positive. For example, when you feel worried, afraid, or anxious, ask yourself: "What's really the worst thing that could happen? How could I deal with that?" Then consider, "What's the best that could happen? What if all goes well?" Focus on what the outcome will look like and feel like. Then channel your energy and enthusiasm toward making things go the way you want.

EMPATHY: To understand others—to walk in their shoes—is to truly hear and understand their thoughts, feelings, and concerns, whether spoken or unspoken. Ask yourself these questions to help gauge your level of empathy and see how you can improve in this EI competency:

→ **WHEN YOU LISTEN,** do you truly pay attention to what the other person is saying? Do you lose focus? Are you thinking about what you can say next?

→ **DO YOU PAY** attention to cues that are verbal (tone of voice, speed, loudness, word choice) and nonverbal (hand gestures, facial expression, posture, eye gaze) to understand what's really being said?

→ **DO YOU MAKE** assumptions?

→ **DO YOU ASK** questions to better understand what the person is saying, feeling, or needing?

→ **DO YOU PROVIDE** feedback—verbal and nonverbal—so that others know you are listening and interested?

By developing these skills and behaviors, you'll improve your ability to manage yourself and interact with others. As a result, you'll distinguish yourself as someone with a well-developed right brain.

RIGHT-BRAIN LEADERSHIP: WHAT GREAT LOOKS LIKE

If you wanted to be a great golfer, you'd probably study how a PGA champion swings—or for basketball, one of the all-time NBA greats. If tennis is your passion, you'd watch every Wimbledon match. Even in our wildest dreams, of course, few of us could probably attain that level of greatness (no matter how much we might wish). But who else would you want to emulate?

We take the same approach when it comes to career advancement. Our researchers have spent years figuring out the skills and traits that have gotten people ahead. Drawing from assessments of nearly 30,000 people at the entry level, mid level, and C level, we compiled high-performance profiles that define what it takes to be great at each of these levels.

Here, we'll look at how greatness is defined in two areas: First, how great leaders handle novel and uncertain situations (*Figure 1*). And second, how great leaders relate to or interact with others (*Figure 2*).

Starting with Figure 1, we can see how the following key traits (most

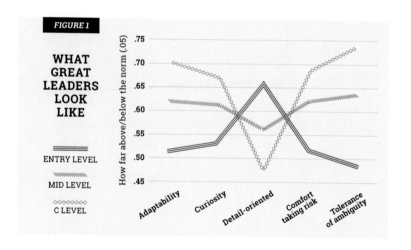

FIGURE 1

WHAT GREAT LEADERS LOOK LIKE

ENTRY LEVEL

MID LEVEL

C LEVEL

How far above/below the norm (.05)

Adaptability · Curiosity · Detail-oriented · Comfort taking risk · Tolerance of ambiguity

Key Leadership Traits

ADAPTABILITY: Being comfortable with unanticipated changes and diverse situations; being able to adjust to constraints and rebound from adversity.

CURIOSITY: Approaching problems in novel ways; seeing patterns and understanding how to synthesize complex information; having the desire to achieve deep understanding.

DETAIL-ORIENTED: Having the ability to systematically carry out tasks as assigned. This left-brain skill helps you understand procedures and the importance of exactitude.

COMFORT TAKING RISKS: Ability to take on and handle risk. (Higher-level positions typically involve more high-risk and high-profile situations.)

TOLERANCE OF AMBIGUITY: Being comfortable with uncertainty and willing to make decisions and plans in the face of incomplete information.

of them right-brain capabilities) relate to performance in the context of handling novel and uncertain situations.

Focusing on the middle of the graph, we can see that being **detail-oriented** is a trait that makes an entry-level person great (remember, it's a left-brain skill). Here, the expectation is that employees will carry out their assigned tasks and responsibilities as instructed. The greater the focus on detail at the entry level, the more coworkers and bosses can count on assignments being completed thoroughly and accurately. In fact, detail orientation is so important, it is the peak for the high-performing entry-level employee.

For the middle manager and especially for the C-level leader, detail orientation appears less pronounced (a lower target to hit), but it remains an important aspect of being an effective leader. These executives are still concerned with the details, knowing that they can make or break any plan or strategy. However, at the mid level and especially at the C level, high performance means successfully delegating to others. A mid-level or senior leader who personally gets bogged down in the details, in fact, is ineffective and will not have the necessary mental bandwidth to focus on strategy.

From entry level to mid level, we see that excellence means ramping up in **adaptability** and **tolerance of ambiguity**, both of which come with experience, particularly involving decision-making and taking on greater responsibility. These two traits are developed even further at the C level, where high-performing leaders must be extremely adaptable and highly tolerant of ambiguity, so they not only react to change but also initiate it.

Finally, at all three levels, **curiosity** is a distinguishing trait. For the high-performing entry-level person, curiosity goes beyond the normal learning curve and includes taking the initiative to soak up new experiences and build new skills. For mid-level managers who distinguish themselves, curiosity leads to competencies in new areas, such as taking on stretch assignments that are almost beyond their capabilities, or immersing themselves in the unfamiliar, such as working in a different country or region. For the C-level leader, curiosity prompts engagement in lifelong learning, which is a prerequisite to greatness.

In Figure 2, we move to the emotional qualities that define high per-

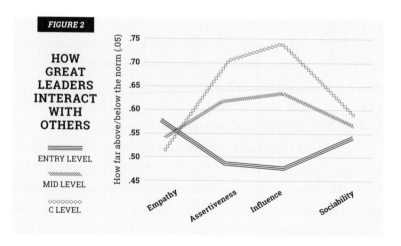

FIGURE 2

HOW GREAT LEADERS INTERACT WITH OTHERS

ENTRY LEVEL
MID LEVEL
C LEVEL

How far above/below the norm (.05)

.75
.70
.65
.60
.55
.50
.45

Empathy   Assertiveness   Influence   Sociability

Right-Brain Emotional Skills

EMPATHY: Having concern for and awareness of others' feelings, problems, and motivations.

ASSERTIVENESS: Enjoying taking charge and directing others; being decisive.

INFLUENCE: Motivating and persuading others; being adept at interpersonal relationships.

SOCIABILITY: Enjoying interactions with others; being energized by the presence of others and easily initiating social interactions.

formance in how people interact with others. As the graph shows, the entry-level person is the mirror opposite of the mid-level manager and the C-level executive in both **assertiveness** and **influence**. While some people are naturally more assertive than others, it is a quality that can be developed with time and experience. For example, you can take on assignments to lead projects and, eventually, to lead people.

Influence, not surprisingly, is a low point for the inexperienced entry-level person, but far more developed for the high-performing middle manager—and a key strength for great leaders. Highly adept C-level leaders leverage their influence and their network to align the team behind unifying goals and a sense of mission.

The two ends of the emotional spectrum as depicted here—**empathy** and **sociability**—show comparatively little difference at all levels. The high-performing entry-level person who must rely on others for coaching and mentoring is very focused on the needs of others—more so than mid-level and C-level leaders. Sociability is nearly equal at the mid level and C level, given the need for these high-performing leaders to interact easily with others. But entry-level people who distinguish themselves are not far behind, displaying people skills that ingratiate them with others and enable them to interact with peers and with colleagues in positions several levels above their own.

THE RIGHT-BRAIN HABIT

Just as you improve your health and wellness by adopting better nutrition and exercise habits—daily, weekly, and monthly routines—you need a similar approach for your right-brain skill development. The following are prompts for self-reflection on a daily, weekly, and monthly basis. Choose the questions that resonate with you—and change it up or add your own later.

FRI
24

GMT-07

5 AM

6 AM

YOUR DAILY DOSE

7 AM

8 AM

9 AM

Each day, reflect on questions that can put your work life into perspective, while building the self-awareness, adaptability, and empathy that comprise right-brain skills.

10 AM
- How have I contributed positivity or negativity to my team and others around me?

11 AM
- What could I do differently to make someone feel better after an interaction they had with me versus how they felt before?

12 PM
- How many times did I say thank you?

1 PM
- How many times did I complain about something or someone?

2 PM
- How did I maintain composure under stress?

- How many new people did I interact with and make a positive impression on today?

3 PM
- Did I listen more—or talk more?

4 PM
- What did I learn today?

5 PM

SUN	MON	TUE	WED	THU	FRI	SAT
28	29	30	31	1	2	3

GMT-07

YOUR WEEKLY WORKOUT

Just as you might devote one day a week to cross-training as part of your fitness routine, pick from the following list of questions to help you exercise your right-brain skills.

- What situations could I have handled differently—not just through my words, but also my nonverbal cues (facial expression, tone, and body language)?
- Which two people will I do something specific for this week?
- What was the best conversation (at work or outside of work) I had this week?
- Whom can I ask for perspective about a challenge or problem I'm facing?
- Whom have I neglected to appreciate out loud?
- What efforts of others have I overlooked?
- Am I more often sharing criticism or praise?
- Have I shared credit with others?

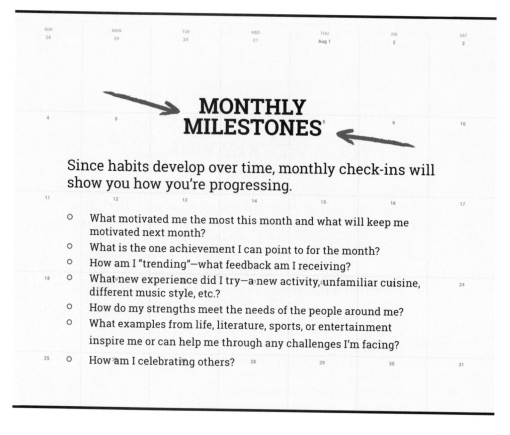

MONTHLY MILESTONES[8]

Since habits develop over time, monthly check-ins will show you how you're progressing.

- What motivated me the most this month and what will keep me motivated next month?
- What is the one achievement I can point to for the month?
- How am I "trending"—what feedback am I receiving?
- What new experience did I try—a new activity, unfamiliar cuisine, different music style, etc.?
- How do my strengths meet the needs of the people around me?
- What examples from life, literature, sports, or entertainment inspire me or can help me through any challenges I'm facing?
- How am I celebrating others?

By becoming more self-reflective and self-aware, you'll understand your true strengths, have the clarity to identify and work on your weaknesses, and achieve a better balance between left brain and right brain.

YOUR 5 TAKEAWAYS

FOR TAPPING
YOUR RIGHT BRAIN

Your left brain got you here; your right brain will take you there.

An IQ of 150 is pointless if your EI is 0.

Self-awareness is the starting point for any skill development and will keep you from derailing.

Developing right-brain skills will help you connect with, influence, and motivate others.

Develop and exercise your right brain with practice and feedback.

Chapter Thirteen

GOING GLOBAL:

The Learning Adventure Begins

So there you are—finally, incredibly, standing in a conference room with "Bon Voyage" scrawled on the whiteboard as your colleagues celebrate your first transfer to an overseas post. You're touched by the thoughtful and expensive bottle of Moutai a friend got you to please your new Chinese clients. Somebody yells out "Speech!" and your mind scrambles for Gettysburg Address–worthy remarks. Suddenly, this voice in your head starts yelling, "What have I done? Why am I uprooting my whole life?

Not to worry. Being nervous over any job transfer is, of course, normal—and it only magnifies when you're shipping yourself and your family 3,000 miles away. Just know that you will hear this voice again, perhaps a lot. Sure, others may brag how they stepped off the plane and never looked back. But the vast majority of people do look back, especially in the first few months. For some, it happens the entire time.

By following the steps in this and every chapter in this book, you understand that you're on a very long-term mission here—to take control of your career and make strong and strategic moves in a way that few people do. Going global is one of those bold moves.

First of all, congratulate yourself. Even getting to this point is quite an accomplishment; it took a lot of work that got you noticed by people above you. Now, those same people are demonstrating a lot of confidence in you by investing in your future and offering an overseas role. No doubt this is a big stage in your career. It's time to flex some new muscles to show how well you can adapt.

Q I've just been given my first expatriate assignment. How can I improve my chances of success?

A Prepare for the learning experience of a lifetime. This is full immersion into the new and different—with a full measure of challenges (personal and professional), frustrations, and adventures. It's a given: learn all you can before you leave. But that's only baseline knowledge. Keep your mind open, drop your biases and preferences for how things should be done, and learn the nuances of the culture, customs, and norms of doing business. Be gracious and respectful—because you're going to make mistakes.

THE
PRELAUNCH
MOVES

Let's go back in time before your going-away party, before you got all pumped (as you should be!) about this amazing next step. It makes sense to pause and engage in research and reflection. That's all part of being the master of your future.

Taking an overseas assignment is, without a doubt, a risky move, whether it's a one-city tour or the first of a series of moves from one country to another. This may be the start of a professional odyssey that takes you from, say, New York to London to Sydney to Dubai and then to Washington, DC. You won't be the same person when it is over, professionally or personally, and neither will many of your colleagues when you return, not to mention the entire company.

Naturally, one of the first things you want to find out when an offer arrives is how long you will be away. Incredibly, this gets lost in the shuffle a lot of times. Is it two years in Europe and back, or unknown? What happens if the company's fortunes change—will it bring you back or keep you in Serbia? Obviously, you can't get a lot of these answers formally in writing, but spelling some of it out in emails with your manager or HR department may be possible. Then there's the issue of what happens when you get back—What position will you get?

Some companies are good at giving out expatriate assignments but not so good at repatriating employees. This can be a major pitfall, especially for younger professionals who fear losing their career momentum. People who have strong client relationships, a well-developed sales territory, or a deep network of internal and external contacts are often afraid of having to start from scratch in a different country where they know only a few people. And what happens to those contacts back home?

Someone else will have to handle that territory and serve those clients.

It's all quite head spinning—and you haven't even gone through the turbulent plane ride across continents to start the new job! My suggestion is to compose a long list of considerations before accepting the offer. Half that list probably centers around personal issues; you may have a spouse or partner who can't move or young children who can't be uprooted from school, which can be deal breakers your company will have to understand. But then there's the professional side; here are several questions to ask:

1 Where will you go?

This isn't as obvious as you think, because the opportunity that arises for you may be in a different city or country than you'd hoped. For example, if you work in investment banking in London, your obvious target is probably to get to New York. But what if the opportunity is in Dallas? Should you take it? Yes! First of all, it accomplishes your main goal of going abroad as an expatriate. Second, once you get to Dallas, it will be far easier to be transferred to New York (after a time and once you've proven yourself) than to wait for a New York expatriate assignment that may not materialize.

2 How is the money?

As you know by now, money is important, but it should never be the sole driving force behind any work decision. That said, cost-of-living differences abroad can be numbing, and even the best HR departments can fail to adjust pay levels fairly. As you might expect,

tax laws are totally different and full of quirks, and healthcare costs (not to mention quality) can vary a lot, too. Research remains your all-important friend and can inform you about any "sticker shock" before it happens.

3 What if the move is lateral?

Even if the money sets you back a bit or leaves you even, and by that measure your international assignment isn't considered a promotion, don't be discouraged. The very fact that you'll be living and working in a different country and global region will make it an enriching experience far beyond your title or scope of duties. Plus, as an expatriate you'll probably have many more opportunities to connect with company executives overseas who are many levels above. The fact is, the ranks are smaller, and your exposure will be greater. These connections will be extremely valuable in the long term as you move around and they do too.

4 ***How long will you stay?***
Your assignment may be specified for one or two years. What if you (or the company) want to extend it? Will the expatriate package, which usually includes allowances for housing, education, and travel back home, extend beyond two years? Or will you be considered a local employee, which could greatly impact your compensation?

5 ***What happens next?***
As I've said, companies can be weak when it comes to welcoming expats back and finding proper roles for them. You want to ask: Will the company reassign you after your first tour or bring you back home? Or will you be on your own to find the next opportunity? It's a conversation that should start while you decide and continue while you are away, as you and your boss assess your contribution and career goals and plans. In some cases, you may be able to devise a plan—but don't be surprised if someday you end up feeling like Tom Hanks in *Castaway*, wondering if you're going to have to build a raft to get back to headquarters.

As you prepare your checklist, always try to keep a larger perspective. An expat assignment really is an amazing experience, but it's not like the rest of the company, including your old department, will be waiting for you. It's akin to when you moved out of your parents' house to go to college and suddenly your old bedroom was converted into the guest room. The point is, your departure for an expat assignment will make room for others back home to move and grow. So don't expect the status quo—for them or yourself—when you return.

CULTURE SHOCK

Even with all the research you've done, once you are abroad you'll probably struggle to fit in. It isn't that others won't be friendly and welcoming, but they have their bonds and habits that connect them. You're bound to be an outsider in the beginning.

A few years ago, when one of my European colleagues was first transferred to the United States with a consulting job in New York, he encountered the Monday-morning office ritual of discussing weekend sports. For my colleague, who associated football with soccer, it was totally foreign— *what was a "down" in football?* Then came spring and baseball—*how long was an "inning," anyway?*

Wanting to bond with the group, he listened and asked questions. He watched the games on the weekend so he could participate in the Monday-morning banter. He knew these social rituals were part of the immersion that would change him from outsider to insider and make him one of the team. It was all part of the complexity of fitting in with the culture, by relying on his intellectual curiosity and genuine desire to know others.

Above all, learn to laugh about yourself. Words and expressions that you misunderstand or that don't translate will create some embarrassment but also offer more opportunities to share a laugh and bond with your colleagues. It's all part of your expatriate learning curve.

THE ULTIMATE LEARNING EXPERIENCE

Maybe the best way to approach your international assignment is to view it as a day-by-day learning experience, the kind that can greatly increase your chances of success. This will keep your guard down and your mind open.

But as we can recall from our college days, the best way to learn quickly is to be mindful of the approach. I can't cover them all, but here are several ways to increase the pace and scope of what you learn to help you assimilate and achieve success faster in an unfamiliar environment.

In the end, going global is exciting but will probably never cease to be a challenge. And that's the whole point. You've chosen to go far outside your comfort zone so you can learn more about the world—and about yourself. That can only happen with full immersion into the new and different that confronts you every day.

You'll never be done learning about a place or a culture and its customs, no matter how long you live there. Embrace the journey!

1 Embrace your new normal. The faster you can assimilate yourself to the new normal, professionally and personally, the better you'll do. Change is constant everywhere—now you've got change on steroids as you adapt to a new country and culture. Expect things to be different. Move away from what you see as the tried-and-true ways things are done back home.

2 Learn to navigate. Awareness is a key survival skill in an international assignment. There will be a lot going on around you, and the speed and complexity of situations will be made further complicated by uncertainty. You need to be able to read what is going on around you and figure out how to navigate it. If you are looking through your own personal lens, you will miss a lot and will likely get caught off guard.

3 Know what to forget. To succeed, you need to know what to forget—and it's probably quite a lot. You know things are going to be different in the way you interact with others and conduct business. You'll probably struggle with this more than you think (most people do—letting go of the familiar can create anxiety). But the faster you can break through your mental barriers, the more easily you'll form fresh connections and gain insights.

4 Focus on both individuals and groups. Colleagues, clients, and neighbors are just a few of the people you will encounter on your expat assignment. They will be both different from you and different from each other. It is best to regard these people as unique individuals who are motivated by different things. Focus on the micro and macro and look for patterns and themes to give you insight into how you should interact and relate to others. The bottom line for most interpersonal relationships is the desire to be seen and understood.

5 Adjust, adjust, and adjust some more. You need to stay on pace with—and ideally ahead of—the changes that confront you. At times, you'll probably feel exhausted by it all. That only means you need more capacity to stretch, since the change isn't going to slow anytime soon. The more effort you put into your mental preparation before you go and while you're there, the better you'll adapt.

6 Deal with ambiguity. International assignments are by their very nature exercises in ambiguity. The farther your situation takes you from what is familiar and understood, the more ambiguous things will get. As you confront near-constant change in an unfamiliar environment, you need to be comfortable with an almost constant lack of clarity. Welcome to ambiguity. Our research reveals that dealing with ambiguity is a very rare competency in the talent marketplace, even though it is one of the most coveted.

7 Embrace diversity. Diversity is valued everywhere. Almost every global company's greatest opportunities are in cultures that are different and more diverse than its home country. The organizations that best embrace diversity and inclusion will be the winners. As you embrace diversity and inclusion, you'll become more emotionally intelligent with a fuller appreciation of how people (individually and in groups) are similar and how they are different. Most importantly, you'll look for ways to leverage these differences to uncover and tap opportunities and problem-solve together.

GOING GLOBAL FROM WHERE YOU ARE

While our focus in this chapter has been on international assignments, be aware that most large companies have many opportunities to gain global exposure while in your current job. If your employer has offices and operations in other countries, that's an invitation to work with and get to know colleagues in other parts of the world. You may never meet them in person, but you can still work closely on assignments and task forces.

For example, your company may be rolling out a product in a new overseas market. If it's part of your job to support that rollout, then great—you have the perfect entrée to increase your understanding of how to serve customers and do business in a different (and geographically distant) market. If it isn't part of what you do every day, you can still be involved, but as something extra to your day-to-day responsibilities. In other words, you volunteer to support a global task force or initiative during off-hours when you aren't doing your regular job.

Yes, you'll be working harder and going well beyond your job description, not to mention losing some sleep and personal or family time because of evening and weekend calls (which you have to assume will never be scheduled with your time zone and sleep in mind). But that's the point of taking control to advance in your career—making selectively important sacrifices for a far greater future for you and your family. You need to find every way possible to learn and stretch in your current role so that you can position yourself for the next opportunity, whether internally or externally. By thinking globally, you'll demonstrate your insights into overseas markets and different ways of conducting business, as well as gleaning broader global knowledge—even though you've never left the home office.

With that, here are four tips for making those virtual global assignments happen:

1 Raise your hand. The best way to get assigned to participate in or support a global initiative is to tell your boss that you're interested. Let your boss know you're willing to take this on in addition to your regular duties and responsibilities. This is also a tangible way of letting your boss know that, one day, you'd like to work abroad. The more you keep this interest top of mind with your boss—even to the point of making it part of your development goals—the greater your chances of getting an international assignment one day. But if you don't get on and stay on your boss's radar for international exposure (and it could take a while), it won't happen.

2 Don't be shy. When your colleagues are also aware of your interest in gaining international exposure, they will be more inclined to tell you about projects or a task force that needs volunteers. And you'll let them know, too, if you hear something that could benefit them. This is part of building your internal network, with give-and-take that helps everyone.

3 Make it good for the company. While working abroad should be a real passion for you, it can't be all about you. Thinking—and one day, going—global is all about expanding your knowledge, skills, and experience so you become a more valuable contributor. You can demonstrate how that global project you're part of makes you even better at delivering on your boss's priorities, especially to connect the dots from team goals to the organization's overarching goals.

4 Broaden your international horizons. The more you interact with your colleagues around the world, the broader your network becomes until it's truly a global network. Now you've broadened your reach both inside and outside the company. To build that network, you lead with what you can give to your international colleagues: your time, expertise, knowledge, and willingness to help. This will require odd hours—early-morning and late-night calls to accommodate their time zones. But if you're passionate about this and you're good at what you do, your input will be welcome. And remember, don't build your professional network in the dark—you can't blindside your boss.

TRAVELING ABROAD

When there are opportunities to travel abroad, you'll probably be one of the few candidates your boss considers sending, because you were the one who participated in all those global assignments and task forces—even when it was on your own time. You've not only proven your interest but earned your way by establishing contacts overseas. That means you can hit the ground running.

Your opportunity to travel abroad may be a weeklong industry conference or sales meeting, which your boss thinks you should attend in person. Or you could be on temporary loan to an international operation for several weeks or even months. The decision to send you probably will have a lot to do with the benefit of having you forge closer ties with colleagues in a different region, share and learn best practices, meet with global customers, and expand your global mindset even more with a boots-on-the-ground experience.

Overcommunicate with Your Boss

If you've been assigned to work for several weeks (or longer) on an assignment overseas, it's hard to know when your boss back home wants to hear from you or receive updates. When in doubt, overcommunicate. That way, there's no question as to what you're doing, what's being accomplished, what challenges you're encountering, and how you should react in specific situations.

This is an exciting next step in the global adventure, because for a period of time—whether measured in days, weeks, or months—you'll no longer be on your own turf. But it's also another one of those moments when the odds of totally messing up are astronomically high, especially if you are unprepared. Overseas travel is challenging at best, and no one has patience with people who miss their flight for a stupid reason like forgetting to update their passport, or miss a meeting by an entire day because they miscalculated the time zone in Beijing. (This happens a lot more than you think!)

Jet lag isn't just a nuisance on overseas trips, it can ruin your career if you zonk out in your hotel room and never make it to see the president of the division who just shelled out five grand to bring you over (again, not so rare). So the alarms need to go off—both literally and in your head—to avoid some of the pitfalls. If you get these logistics down, I promise the payoffs will be worth it. You'll be getting a chance to connect in person with colleagues and customers who have gotten to know you by name and voice but never had a chance to meet you until now. Indeed, there's nothing like business travel for building and reinforcing your global network.

HARD-WON WISDOM

(Usually from Less-Than-Pleasant Experiences)

NEVER, EVER CHECK YOUR BAGS.

You want your stuff with you at all times. I was en route to Madrid with a connection in London's Heathrow Airport. Except the flight was diverted because of a snowstorm and we landed somewhere in Ireland. The airline told us we'd be stuck there for 14 hours because the pilot and crew had exceeded their legal flying time. While everyone waited in the tiniest airport terminal with their bags still on board the plane, I grabbed my carry-ons, rented a car, and drove through Ireland along country roads to the city of Cork. I got a seat on a cheap regional airline (back row, middle seat—of course), and landed at Heathrow around midnight. I stayed at an airport hotel with all the ambience of a minimum-security prison and got up at 4:30 in the morning

CONTINUED

to catch the flight to Madrid. But I made it on time, and all because I had my bags with me.

IT ISN'T NEW YEAR'S EVE.

Just because you're stuck on an airplane for six or eight hours (or more), you can't decide that it's New Year's Eve. Crossing the Atlantic is not the time for five gin and tonics. Instead, drink water. Flying dehydrates you, so you can't drink enough water. And speaking of water, when you're on the ground, it's bottled water all the way, even when you brush your teeth.

NEVER TAKE A NAP.

The jet lag will kill you (London is eight hours ahead of Los Angeles— brutal). No matter how tired you are, don't nap. If you do, you'll wake up in the middle of the night and stare at the ceiling until daybreak. Better to force yourself to adjust to the new time. Stay up until midnight, even if by that point you're slurring your words and starting to drool.

DON'T EAT FOOD THAT'S WAVING AT YOU.

It isn't that the food is bad, you're just not used to it. So while you might like to try that delicacy that's all tentacles waving at you, think twice. Stick with what's cooked and familiar—your stomach will thank you. And never eat food from a street vendor. If you do, prepare to "revisit" that decision (again and again) at 38,000 feet on the flight home.

TAKE THE MEDICINE CABINET WITH YOU.

This is one I learned the hard way. I was in China, giving a speech, when I began to feel ill. As soon as I finished the speech, I ran from the stage, sure I was going to vomit. What followed was days of being in my hotel room, seen by three sets of doctors who didn't speak English (I had to show them pictures on the internet to try to explain my various gastrointestinal problems.) I ended up on an IV in my hotel room. Finally, I was able to convince the airline to let me fly (I was so sick they had refused me at first), and it was a rough flight home. After that, I made it a rule: fly with a bag of medicine. And if your company offers international travel insurance,

use it—just in case you need to be evacuated after a serious illness or accident.

BE NICE TO CUSTOMS.

And while we're on the topic of unpleasantness while traveling, let me share that I've been strip-searched a few times. The last time was in Canada, after I had made three trips in three weeks while our firm was making an acquisition. When customs asked about it, though, they may not have liked my answer. Or maybe I had a little attitude. What followed was about six hours by myself in a room and a strip search. Not fun. Be nice to customs. Follow all the rules, answer the questions, and don't put duty-free in your suitcase.

YOUR 5 TAKEAWAYS

FOR GOING GLOBAL

Before leaving, know exactly what you're getting into, how long it will last, and how you will get home again. In other words, negotiate your way out of your expat assignment as you negotiate your way in.

Lead with both your intellectual and emotional curiosity, along with self-confidence in your ability to be flexible and adapt.

Know that no matter how much you study and prepare, you will make countless mistakes, especially at first.

Rely on your colleagues to coach and guide you. They're your lifeline.

Immerse yourself in local social rituals.

Chapter Fourteen

LEARNING IT ALL:

Do Rabbits Scream?

It's the secret to sustainable success:
if you're happy, you're motivated, and
if you're motivated, you're going to outperform. And a large driver of being
happy and motivated can be learning. If
you're learning, you're probably growing.

This may come as a surprise, but think
about it—learning is the pathway to bigger
and better opportunities, and that translates
into greater engagement and having the
satisfaction that you're making a difference.

In my mind, the people who aren't trying to learn on the job are actually at the most risk of being miserable. They hate their work, but the problem is more than the usual suspects—a boorish boss, a horrible commute, a dysfunctional department. The root cause of their sadness is the rut they've created. Research bears this out: according to Korn Ferry's global employee opinion database, 76 percent of employees who feel intrinsically motivated exceed their performance expectations, compared to 60 percent for those who feel extrinsically motivated.

And there are extrinsic benefits, too. Learning is the number one determinant of how much you'll earn over your career. That's why every job you take should come with ample learning opportunities, so that you're better positioned for the next move and the one after that. People who are curious and take risks are often the best learners. Until you experience challenging job tasks where you must perform and face a real risk of failing, you will not develop significantly.

This is the essence of learning from experience. And by learning, we're talking about advancing your skill sets, grasping whole new concepts

Q My company doesn't offer much in terms of formal training. How can I learn more?

A Keep in mind the 70-20-10 rule of thumb. Formal training accounts for only about 10 percent of development; 70 percent is from on-the-job experiences, and 20 percent is from other people, such as your boss. Learning and development occur in first-time situations and difficult challenges. Look for ways to stretch and grow by volunteering for new assignments and going outside your comfort zone. There's nothing like a complex problem or a good crisis to accelerate your learning.

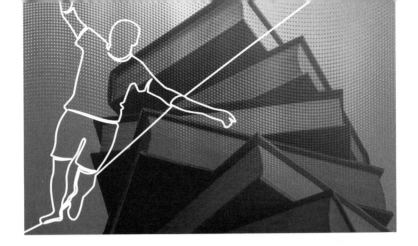

about business, and moving up the emotional intelligence ladder.

In today's world, you should be having multiple learning experiences—some you get by nagging your boss or pushing your company, others by driving yourself. Think of it as a mini degree. Sure, it won't have a "summa cum laude" or university logo on it. But it will signal to you that you put the time and effort into every gig and came away each time just a little bit smarter and more prepared for whatever lies ahead.

Not that learning on the job didn't matter in previous generations, but schooling yourself at work is all the more important since you probably won't be staying at one company more than a few years in the nomad economy we've discussed. Plus, no matter how hard you work, no matter how great your performance reviews are, companies in the global economy may downsize entire departments—and their staffs—with little warning. If you haven't advanced your skill set, you could be dead in the water if that happens.

So if you take away nothing else from this chapter, here's the big message: the main considerations for any job you take, more than your title and even your salary, are what you are learning and who you are learning from. That could be your current boss, your future boss, or even your colleagues.

Too bad "Steve" didn't realize this until it was too late. By the time he reached out to me through a mutual friend for some advice, there wasn't much I could tell him other than the painful truth. The job opportunity he had just turned down was "the one that got away."

Here's what happened: Steve started getting calls from an in-house recruiter at a company he knew about a big job with room to grow, but with only a modest salary increase. He was interested, at least at first, but after thinking about it, he decided he was comfortable with where he was. Steve knew this new job would require longer hours, more travel, and worst of all, he would be the new guy and have to prove himself all over again.

The recruiter called one last time, but Steve basically said, "Thanks, but no thanks." His decision to stay wasn't because of his analysis of opportunities based on where he could stretch himself, learn more, and reset his career trajectory. Rather, Steve's fear of failure led him to inflate the potential risks that come with trying something new. In the end, his complacency and fear made him call off this promising job opportunity.

STEVE'S FEAR OF FAILURE LED HIM TO INFLATE THE POTENTIAL RISKS.

Flash-forward six months: Steve's feelings of being comfortable in his old job morphed into boredom. Every day felt the same, and regret nagged him as he thought back on that lost job opportunity. Worse yet, after another three months passed, the unthinkable happened: Steve was "downsized." When he contacted that internal recruiter to say his circumstances had changed and he was interested in pursuing a job, he received a rather cool response about "no opportunities at the present time." That's when Steve reached out to me, but there wasn't much I could do other than tell him what he already knew: he clearly had burned a bridge. If only he had grasped the opportunity to take control.

Complacency killed Steve's chances—as it can kill all careers. Know this: you may be well paid now and comfortable in your position, but if you aren't being challenged to learn and grow, you aren't doing yourself any favors. If you aren't learning, it's time to take control.

A great tool for making this determination is what I call the "Learn It or Leave It" checklist. It's a real litmus test for judging whether you should stay in your current job or seek another opportunity to be better positioned for the future:

Is your work meaningful?

Are you engaged in what you're doing? Does the organization you work for have a mission/vision/purpose that you can support and feel aligned with?

Who are you working for?

Are you working for a boss who champions you, who wants to help you grow and develop with challenging assignments?

Are you learning?

What new skills are you gaining? While it's impossible to predict the skills that will be needed in the future, one thing is certain: if you don't learn, you won't grow, and if you don't grow, you'll never progress.

LIFELONG
LEARNING

As you grasp the concept of learning while working, you will hear about the idea of "lifelong learning." This takes a lot of focus and stamina; learning is hard. For generation after generation, most people figured they were done learning when they finished college or maybe business school. But the goal now is to learn continuously with a lifetime of new challenges, direct feedback, and self-reflection.

Once again, we meet the 70-20-10 formula of career advancement. To review, 70 percent of your learning will happen on the job, including stretch assignments and challenging tasks; 20 percent will come from other people, including your boss; and only 10 percent will come from formal training. Given this proportion, it's clear you must get out of your comfort zone.

Lifelong learning is a process, and given the changing demographics of today's multigenerational workforce, no one can say how that process works for any one person. To be sure, we know that how long people can or should work is no longer determined by the views of the past. Those ideas and assumptions are less relevant, especially as life expectancy expands to the triple digits. One day, age 50 or 60 could very well be the midpoint for one's career or the opportune time to switch from one professional discipline to another. Imagine career longevity as the norm and not the exception.

EVOLVE OR BECOME PROFESSIONALLY EXTINCT.

The workplace of the future will take age diversity to another level, with potentially five generations working side by side.

Exponentially expanding careers pose an even greater need for continuous learning in order for workers to be relevant for a longer period of time. More and more, people will have careers that evolve with changes in the global marketplace and the rapid explosion of technology. This means keeping pace by expanding one's skills, competencies, and experiences.

Being adaptable means not only being able to swipe left and swipe right, but also learning and applying lessons from the past to the present (otherwise known as learning agility, which we'll discuss in more depth later in this chapter). "Evolve or become professionally extinct" is the Darwinian rule of today's workforce.

WHAT LEARNERS LOOK LIKE

We've all meet the Steves of the world, so we know what people who are not learning look and act like. Now, let's look at the people who *do* want to learn.

✔ **Learners are willing to feel and look stupid.** This is the only way to learn and perform well in new situations. Admit what you don't know. You know you're not an expert, but you want to develop expertise and become known for something.

✔ **Learners are world-class observers of themselves, others, and situations.** You know that wise voice we all have that sits on our shoulder and gives advice to us all the time? With learners, that voice is objective and dispassionate: What's going on here? How are people reacting? Why? What's working? What isn't? Is there anything I can take away that is repeatable?

✔ **Learners know that more is better.** Learners have more ways to handle situations because they have more conscious learning tactics. They will try anything; they'll keep a journal, write down a plan, or engage in a visioning exercise.

✔ **Learners make comparisons.** Learners will search the past for parallels, whether that means asking others in the company or reading a biography. They know there is nothing new and that history repeats itself, if only in broad themes.

✔ **Learners make sense through rules of thumb.** Many learners keep lists, mental or written, of things that might be true most of the time. These are guiding principles and trends they use to view situations.

✔ **Learners are likely to have a plan and measures of success and failure.** Learners evaluate what they did, decide what worked, and understand why it worked. With this information, they try again and again. The more tries they have, the more chances there are to learn to get it right.

LEARNING AGILITY

Our focus on learning highlights a very important trait: learning agility, which Korn Ferry considers to be the key determinant of professional success. This trait speaks to your willingness and ability to apply lessons learned from past experiences to new situations and challenges. As I said, I think of it as knowing what to do when you don't know what to do.

Highly learning-agile people tend to have desirable qualities for tomorrow's economy: dealing well with (and actually enjoying) ambiguity and complexity; being reflective and insightful; embracing new things and different approaches; and willingly assuming accountability and ultimate responsibility, particularly when things fail. They move beyond the status quo and focus on reinvention.

LEARNING AGILITY ENCOMPASSES FOUR ASPECTS:

SELF-AWARENESS:
You are reflective, understand your strengths and blind spots, and seek feedback and personal insight. This is "knowing thyself," which is the prerequisite to any learning and advancement (see Chapter Twelve, "Tapping Your Right Brain").

MENTAL AGILITY:
You embrace complexity, examine problems in unique ways, make fresh connections, and stay inquisitive. If you're high in mental agility, you're not only capable

of working through uncertainty, you actually embrace and get excited by it. With mental agility, you're curious, have a wide range of interests, and read broadly across a wide range of topics. You're comfortable with ambiguity and can easily identify parallels and contrasts.

PEOPLE AGILITY:
You listen first and are open to diverse viewpoints. You challenge preconceived notions and use your emotional intelligence to uncover your

unconscious biases and address them. When meeting someone for the first time, you refrain from making snap decisions during those crucial first seven seconds. Instead, you suspend judgment and keep an open mind.

CHANGE AGILITY:
With change agility, you continuously explore new options. It's never "this is the way we've always done things." You're good at devising what-if scenarios. You can go from idea to implementation.

Four Signs You're Learning Agile

1 You know yourself.
2 You are curious about the world.
3 You listen first and ask why second.
4 You are willing to fail.

By becoming more agile in every dimension, you'll be better prepared and more confident when challenging the status quo.

One of the best examples of knowing what to do when you don't know what to do happened on a flight not so long ago from Hawaii back to Los Angeles. We were already in our seats when the pilot boarded the plane. He wore a short-sleeve shirt, unbuttoned at the neck, and his hair was a little on the longer side. Strapped to his flight bags was a guitar. "What are you going to play?" I asked him.

"Dylan," he replied with a smile.

"Oh, I love Dylan," I told him. A moment later I turned to my daughter: "This is going to be an interesting flight."

In the middle of this routine flight, with clear skies and no turbulence, our plane made an emergency evasive move—a 600-foot dive in a matter of seconds. Those gut-churning seconds felt like an hour on a runaway roller coaster, with a sharp drop that put my stomach in my mouth. During the dive, some of the passengers screamed. When the plane stabilized, the fear was visible on the faces of passengers and flight attendants alike. Then came the eerie silence as we waited for what came next.

After what felt like hours, the copilot made an announcement on the PA system in that police/military speak—something about another aircraft being in our airspace. I told my daughter, "You know what that means—we almost had a head-on collision."

Then out came the beverage carts and it was free-booze time. The woman in front of me threw back two mini bottles of Jack Daniel's. By the time the plane landed, most people had forgotten all about the Pacific Ocean.

Flash forward a week: While I was watching the news, a segment came on about a heroic pilot who averted what could have been the deadliest midair collision in history over the Pacific Ocean. I sat there, stunned. That was our plane!

The hero was that laid-back, Dylan-playing pilot, who navigated in the moment because of his training, which had honed his skills to the point of becoming instinctive.

Adversity: The Best Teacher

If you want to develop your agility, nothing is a better teacher than adversity or discomfort. Add in some failure—failing fast and learning faster—and you'll greatly improve your ability to see things in a new light and search for different answers and solutions.

How Learning Agile Are You?

To get an indication of how learning agile you are, take the following quiz. At the end, add up the points for each response and compare to the scoring key.

10–20 points
Your pattern of scores indicates a predisposition toward "learning agility"—especially change agility and mental agility. The ability to deal with uncertainty and change, while having the capacity to tolerate a lack of details, is a hallmark of the agile approach to work.

21–30 points
Your pattern of scores indicates a predisposition toward diligence and dutifulness. Detail orientation and a need for certainty are hallmarks of a strong contributing employee, but they can impede promotion and are in many ways the opposite of an agile approach to work.

1 POINT ▶
Strongly Disagree

2 POINTS ▶
Disagree

3 POINTS ▶
Agree

1   It's important that I attend to every detail.   [   ]

2   I accept nothing less than perfection.   [   ]

3   The work isn't finished until every detail has been worked out with due diligence.   [   ]

4   Rules are not meant to be broken.   [   ]

5   I work best when goals and solutions are clear.   [   ]

6   Stability and clarity are key to a successful career.   [   ]

7   Flexibility leads to mistakes.   [   ]

8   I always strive to achieve certainty so that work is done correctly.   [   ]

9   Making decisions without full information is bad for the company.   [   ]

10   It's important to achieve a stable and reliable work environment.   [   ]

WHO IS TEACHING YOU?

You are the company you keep. Unfortunately, it's easy to slip to the lowest common denominator. The only way to get better is to surround yourself with people who will challenge you. It's like in sports—when you're up against better players, you'll lose at first; but in time, you'll up your game. It's the same thing in the workplace: seek to learn from and model the high performers—people who are better at what they do than you are.

Ideally this means your boss, who is often the best person to learn from. Think about it: Who but your boss has the context of your current job responsibilities, your strengths and weaknesses, and how you need to stretch and grow to expand your contribution? So when you choose the boss you'll be working for, choose wisely. Remember, your boss has control over 90 percent of your learning in the 70-20-10 formula (the 70 percent from on-the-job experiences and 20 percent from other people).

The unfortunate reality, though, is that even if you have a good boss, he or she may not be a great mentor. If that's the case, you need to find a mentor elsewhere. This is a person who understands your day-to-day job, your career development, and your ambitions. Don't confuse this person with a coach, who is outside the company and can give you objective feedback on yourself and your strategy (see Chapter Eleven, "Networking Within"). Rather, a mentor can show you the ropes inside the organization, offer advice for getting stretch assignments and development opportunities, and help you network.

No matter whom you learn from, the best teacher is your experiences.

EIGHT CAREER-BUILDER IMPERATIVES

Embracing new experiences highlights the importance of learning and development opportunities.
Whether these experiences occur in the world, on the job, or in formal programs, they provide opportunities for enrichment, exploration, and engagement. Continuously responding to novel experiences also builds your capacity for agility.

Adopting deliberate practice and reflection will help you acquire complex skills.
Deliberate practice involves setting specific goals and making small changes in behavior based on feedback and monitoring your outcomes.

Learning from others reflects the 70-20-10 rule and the importance of learning through relationships.
Having a mentor or a supportive boss who champions you will help you gain more learning.

Fostering a growth mindset reminds you of the change that occurs only when you let go of what you followed or valued in the past and redefine yourself in some new ways.
A growth mindset will help you overcome resistance to change and an unconscious addiction to the familiar.

Leveraging emotion speaks to the importance of emotion in helping you learn.
As studies show, we remember not only facts but the feelings associated with them. Emotion also facilitates development by fueling motivation. The more you understand your own emotions, the better you can recognize and understand others.

Optimizing stress encourages opportunities to move out of your comfort zone and into learning opportunities.
Constructive stress can help you stretch and grow in response to challenges.

Practicing mindfulness taps an inner state in which you can observe yourself in action.
Instead of reacting automatically, you use mindfulness to create a space between a stimulus and your reaction. Mindfulness can empower you and allow you to assume greater responsibility in your life.

Enacting behavioral commitments allows you to tap powerful drivers of personal change.
Behavioral commitments set expectations for how you will act, react, and interact with others. With each commitment, you can change the dynamic in the moment and reinforce productive behavior.

By using these eight imperatives systematically, consistently, and in combination, you will increase your chances of creating and sustaining the kind of change that will increase your development and help secure your career trajectory.

THE AWAKENING

One final story—a tale of changing faulty assumptions, learning from experience, and knowing what to do when you don't know what to do.

It was 1:35 in the morning and I was sound asleep when my wife, Leslie, woke me up. "There's something outside, and it's stuck in our fence."

Fully awake, I got dressed and grabbed a flashlight. Charlie, our golden retriever puppy, was going crazy. When I opened the door, I knew why. A high-pitched scream, like nothing I'd ever heard, sent a chill right through me. Any coyotes in the area were surely on the alert for a trapped animal—but what?

I followed that awful sound to the fence around our property, where I discovered the source of that penetrating shriek.

A rabbit.

This was the last thing I expected. I'd always thought of rabbits as timid and docile ... and silent. If someone told me that rabbits could scream, I wouldn't have believed it. For $1,000 in the *Jeopardy!* category of "Animals Making Loud Noises," I would guess lions, tigers, and elephants. Rabbits? Not a chance.

But firsthand experience (the 70 in the 70-20-10) is always the best teacher. It takes an open mind and a willingness to reexamine biases to overcome assumptions.

After my awakening realization, I still had a stuck bunny to deal with. Wearing heavy gloves, I tried to untangle the rabbit, but it kept squirming and screaming. After a few attempts to free its leg, I went to the garage for some tools and came back with cutters. I cut the fencing and that rabbit shot out of there. All was quiet again.

YOUR **5** TAKEAWAYS

FOR BECOMING A LEARN-IT-ALL

Learning determines your earnings for life—and learning can be as simple as following good old-fashioned curiosity.

Lifelong learning means failing fast (and learning faster).

Learning generally only happens when you're outside your comfort zone.

Learning agility—applying past lessons and experiences to new and first-time challenges and situations—will help you handle ambiguity and complexity and find new and innovative solutions.

Purposefully surround yourself with people who are better than you.

THE 90-DAY CAREER DIET

IN THIS ERA OF THE CAREER NOMAD, you won't be in just one job for life. Every few years you'll look to make a move, whether inside or outside your company. The 90-Day Career Diet takes you through the essential steps to land that next job. This three-month plan will help you recharge professionally and adopt new lifelong habits.

STEP 1

LEARN ABOUT YOURSELF

When undertaking any major change, you need to start by assessing where you are now. For dieters who want to get healthier that means body mass index (BMI), cholesterol, blood pressure, etc. Careers, too, have their own health statistics, which come together in your CMI—Career Momentum Index. Here are a few questions to consider for measuring your CMI:

ARE YOU ENGAGED IN YOUR CURRENT JOB? Do you wake up every morning ready to go, or do you hit the snooze button—literally and figuratively?

DOES YOUR BOSS RECOGNIZE YOUR CONTRIBUTIONS? When was the last time your boss acknowledged what you do? How well did you do on your last performance review—have you even had one in the last 12 months?

ARE YOU CONSIDERED INDISPENSABLE? Are you the go-to person for your boss and the team, who does whatever it takes to get things done?

WHEN WAS THE LAST TIME YOU WERE PROMOTED? Two years ago? Five years ago? Longer?

WHEN WAS THE LAST TIME YOU LEARNED SOMETHING NEW IN YOUR JOB? Are you stretching and growing, or is it the same old, same old every day?

If you're honest with yourself, the answers to these questions may be quite sobering. Maybe you've settled into complacency, which can creep up on you without warning just like those 15 pounds you gained without really knowing when. Same thing for your career: you're in the same job, passed over for promotion. You become sluggish and unmotivated.

But it doesn't have to stay that way.

Whether you're trying to get healthier or get your career in shape, the parallels are unmistakable: you need discipline and new habits. And just like you have a gym membership to get your body into shape, you need a plan and coaching to get your career into shape.

Your Homework
A GOOD LOOK IN THE MIRROR

To begin, **you must be self-aware** and gain perspective about yourself: your strengths and weaknesses, your skills and experiences, what you're passionate about, your sense of purpose, what motivates you, and how you can make a greater difference to your current or future employer.

An assessment of who you are and what you bring to your job can be viewed through four lenses: traits, drivers, competencies, and experiences. Here's a quick look at each and how you can gain deeper insight into who you are and what you do.

WHO YOU ARE

TRAITS:
Hardwired parts of your makeup that are mostly inborn and define who you are:

→ Are you more assertive or passive?

→ Do you embrace or avoid risk-taking?

→ How confident are you in what you know and what you can do?

DRIVERS:
What motivates you—your purpose and passion. Your drivers will tell you what kind of company culture and environment and what type of boss fit you best. For example, which of these are you motivated by?

→ **Challenge:** Overcoming obstacles and taking on tough assignments

→ **Power:** Achieving work-related status and influence, with greater visibility in the organization

→ **Independence:** Taking an entrepreneurial approach, with greater freedom from organizational constraints to pursue your own vision

→ **Collaboration:** Working interdependently to pursue goals in a group to achieve work-related success

WHAT YOU DO

COMPETENCIES:
The skills and abilities you possess that are essential to your success:

→ Would you describe yourself as resourceful, courageous, innovative, and/or adaptable?

→ Can you manage ambiguity, dealing with the unforeseen and moving forward when the way is not clear?

→ Are you a lifelong learner who is insatiably curious and open to new situations and challenges?

EXPERIENCE:
The story you tell based on what you've accomplished. Not only will this help you write a resume, it will also help you become more fluent in communicating your accomplishments.

→ Can you identify accomplishments in your current job?

→ What results do you achieve or contribute meaningfully to?

Your Stretch Assignment
KNOW THYSELF EVEN BETTER

In addition to self-assessing, you can take the next step into greater self-knowledge by completing a formal assessment. A career coach can administer this to you, or you can find resources online.

Another way is to get 360-degree feedback on how people see you. Ask your current and past bosses, colleagues, and others who work with you. Tell them you want honest input on your strengths and areas where you need development. A good question to ask a former boss is, "If I were working for you now, what position would you see me in?"

SELF-KNOWLEDGE
TO SUCCESS

With better self-knowledge through honest self-assessment, you'll be on your way to getting your career in shape. But don't mistake the assessment for the end goal: it isn't just the insight you gain, but what you do with it—just like having a gym membership and buying new running shoes won't guarantee that you'll reach your fitness goals unless you use them! The key to the 90-Day Career Diet is becoming disciplined and developing new habits that empower you to attain and sustain greater career success.

STEP 2

SET YOUR TARGETS

You haven't had a raise in two years—nor a promotion. Most telling, nobody has said thank you for the work you've done. All of this adds up to a negative Career Momentum Index. Just like you need new nutrition and exercise habits to improve your BMI, you must work to optimize your CMI.

The sad reality is, most people don't know how. All of those plans to find a new job, and the Post-its stuck all over the house as reminders, will be fruitless. Why? Because people default to sending out resumes blindly and clicking to apply for any and all job openings—oblivious to the fact that 98 percent of resumes submitted online go nowhere.

You need to take control. But you have to do it within the context of a "career nomad" strategy—taking control as you go from one opportunity to the next, whether inside or outside your current company.

Your Homework
TARGETING QUESTIONS

To target your next opportunity, you need to start with the basics. But believe me, these aren't just "check the box" questions. You need to do some real research.

WHAT ARE YOUR SKILLS AND COMPETENCIES?
Your skills and competencies are a significant part of what you bring to your next position—whether inside or outside your current workplace. What has made you successful thus far? Do you have strong financial acumen? Are you naturally creative? Can you motivate others? How do you drive results?

WHAT ROLES AND RESPONSIBILITIES FIT YOU BEST?
Your search is like a spiral. If you're looking to do the same job for a similar company—maybe with a little more responsibility or a bigger team— it's just one turn on the spiral. If you want to make a bigger leap, perhaps changing industries, that will take you farther out on the spiral. Whatever your plan, you need to translate your experiences and accomplishments to the roles you're seeking.

WHERE DO YOU WANT TO LIVE AND WORK?
Don't tell a prospective employer that you can go anywhere unless that's really the truth. The company isn't going to move—you are. Have a geographic region in mind: Do you need to be in or near a specific city? That two-hour commute each way will get old really fast. Be honest with yourself.

WHAT COMPANIES INTEREST YOU?
Your wish list starts with companies you admire for their purpose and mission—places where you could really see yourself working. Average job tenure is about four years, and a lot less for young professionals. You need to think in short-term increments.

Your Stretch Assignment
THE DEEPER DIVE

The next step is taking a deeper dive into your targeted companies— although, quite frankly, most people won't, because it takes time and effort. Do yourself a favor and don't shortchange your research.

CHECK OUT THE PEOPLE LANDSCAPE. Go on LinkedIn and check out people at your target company. Are you connected to any of them? How long have they been there? Whom do they report to? Does it appear to be a small or a large department? Where did the people come from—what are their qualifications? Do their profiles indicate that they've been promoted along the way? You won't get a complete org chart by any means, but you'll get a good view of the landscape within the company and department and around the specific role(s) you're interested in.

DO THE DUE DILIGENCE. Read the latest news stories about the company. Check out their social media. Read the annual report. Listen to the latest earnings-call recording. Here are some things to consider:

> → **What's the health of the company?** Is it growing, stagnant, shrinking? What's the industry like?

> → **What's the company's reputation?** You're looking for an employer that's known for its brands, its products/services, and the way it does business. Look at websites dedicated to company reputations. What are current and former employees saying? Is the company known for treating employees well? What are the compensation and benefits like? Has the employer been recognized on any lists as a best place to work? Is it known for corporate social responsibility?

> → **What's the culture?** Talk to people who currently work at the company or were there recently. It's all about finding where you can do your best work, make an impact, and prove your value fast.

> → **How's the fit?** Is it a yoga-pants-and-hoodies kind of place, or is it more buttoned down? Consider that most people are hired for what they know but fired for who they are. Make sure who you are fits where you want to go.

SHARPENING YOUR FOCUS ON THE TARGET

As you target companies, think about what's most important to you. Be honest with yourself about your desires and your limitations. The clearer you are about what you need, the better you'll be able to target your next advancement opportunity.

STEP 3

NURTURE YOUR NETWORK

Somebody knows someone who knows somebody who knows you. That's the power of networking as you continue on your 90-Day Career Diet. In previous steps, we've covered the importance of knowing yourself (strengths and weaknesses, passion and purpose) and of targeting opportunities by identifying the industries, companies, and roles that most interest you. Now it's time for the next step—networking your way to a warm introduction.

Most people are terrible at networking. Some are shy about asking for help, but more people ask for help inappropriately. If you haven't seen or spoken to someone for five or 10 years and you suddenly bombard them with requests for help getting a job, that's not networking—it's an ambush!

I've been the recipient of guerrilla networking once from an anesthesiologist while I was undergoing a very minor procedure and once from a dry cleaner who slipped her son's resume into my shirts. Another time, a person I barely knew more than two decades earlier demanded that I help him get a job on his release from prison after doing time for a white-collar crime. Needless to say, this isn't effective.

Most of us need to network to be validated by another person—unlike the select few whose background is all the entrée they need: the Harvard graduate, the West Point graduate, the Navy SEAL, the professional athlete, etc.

Keep in mind that no one is going to vouch for you unless he or she knows you. But when you find someone who is willing to put in a good word for you with the HR department or the hiring manager, you'll be so much further ahead than the other candidates seeking the same position. In the best possible scenario, your contact is so enthusiastic about you that a prospective employer is willing to create a position just to have you join the team.

It goes without saying that you must have a robust network, built and nurtured on the basis of what you can do for others. Let's assume you've done that—although if not, be aware: you can't take out what you haven't put in. Now is a perfect time to start reaching out to people—not with any agenda, just to reconnect. With a healthy network, you're well positioned to tap your network and to navigate the six degrees of separation between you and the somebody who knows somebody at your target companies.

WHOM DO YOU KNOW?

START BY LISTING EVERYONE YOU KNOW:
family members, friends, current and former colleagues, business contacts, members of professional organizations, and people you know socially or through groups you belong to. Think about people you see regularly.

→ **Former bosses and former colleagues** know you from working and interacting with you. Former bosses, in particular, can attest to your skills, accomplishments, and contributions as a team member or team leader. Where are they now? Where have their career paths taken them? Are any working at companies that you wish to target in your job search? And who knows— they may even be looking to fill a position that would be perfect for you.

→ **Peers and former classmates are great sources** of information about different industries, companies, and roles. These contacts have great insights based on their own experiences at different companies (e.g., how work gets done). And those who know you well can probably provide meaningful feedback on where you'd be a good fit.

→ **Family and friends may be the most inclined to help,** especially to reach others within their networks. Younger professionals, in particular, can engage in what I call vertical networking by tapping into their parents' networks. Yet beware: don't ask to connect with more senior people without knowing exactly what you're looking for. Are you seeking insights into a company or industry? Do you want to know about someone's career path? People will be far more interested in sharing this information than in suddenly being asked to help you get a job.

Your Homework

TAPPING THE NETWORK

To make your networking count, you need to do your homework:

SET A GOAL
so your discussions with people have a purpose. The more that people understand what you need and what you're asking, the better they can help you.

CATEGORIZE YOUR CONTACTS
while thinking about the companies at the top of your wish list of future employers. Who in your network can connect you to those organizations?

BE RESPECTFUL
of other people's time. Whether you're reaching out to pick someone's brain or requesting an introduction, that person is doing you a favor.

Your Stretch Assignment

NETWORKING TO FIND REFERENCES

It's one thing to find people who can help make an introduction for you and quite another to identify people who can vouch for you. Companies often engage in deep due diligence (especially for senior positions) when it comes to checking references, both listed and unlisted. Long before you're asked to provide references, know who they are.

→ *Who can comment substantively about you?* Don't choose references just because they're likely to say good things about you. Identify people who can comment substantively about you, how you work, and how you interact with and lead others.

→ *What would former bosses say?* Do you have former bosses or supervisors in your network? (It helps if you've been actively networking with them all along.) Let your former boss or supervisor know you're engaging in some career exploration. Given your experience and skill set, what does your former boss think is a logical next step for you? This type of networking contributes to your ongoing self-assessment while also helping you identify references who can speak meaningfully about your strengths and weaknesses.

If you've taken the time to build and nurture your network, you have a great asset at your disposal: people who are ready and willing to put in a good word for you. Then it's up to you to make the next step.

STEP 4

REFRESH YOUR RESUME

Your resume isn't an epitaph for what you've done in the past. It's a living document that, when coupled with your LinkedIn profile, can generate real enthusiasm.

There's a reason why I'm addressing the resume now, in this fourth step of the 90-Day Career Diet. Your resume alone is not the gateway to a new job. People think it accounts for 90 percent, but it's really only 10 percent. Far more important are targeting your next opportunities and networking your way to a warm introduction. That said, having a fresh and relevant resume will help keep your momentum.

Taking a living-document approach achieves two important goals:

REAL-TIME RESUME.

First, you capture an expanded role or new accomplishments while they're still fresh in your mind. Did you finish the past year 12 percent above plan? Update your resume with that fact. In the new year, have you been assigned to a team launching a new marketing campaign to expand from B2B to B2C? Capture that in a few sentences on your resume. Recording your accomplishments as you achieve them is far easier than trying to remember everything five years later.

LINKEDIN UPDATES.

Second, your living-document approach translates into another important platform: your LinkedIn profile or other professional social media presence. The fact is, the resume has lost a lot of its weight over the years to the LinkedIn profile. Recruiters and hiring managers will check you out online; typically, it's one of the first things they do. Leveraging the living-document strategy will keep both your resume and your professional social media up to date. Importantly, this will also ensure there are no significant differences between your resume and your LinkedIn profile. Any discrepancies can be a major red flag.

Your Homework

DELVING INTO THE DETAILS

Updating your resume or LinkedIn profile is time-consuming, so you may be tempted to procrastinate. Or you get paralyzed in the details—should you use Times New Roman or Calibri? Is "can-do attitude" a noun or an adjective? And all of a sudden you think you're the Hemingway of resumes. Don't do this to yourself! The first new overhaul will involve some work, but with a living-document approach it becomes far less painful going forward.

If you ask five people for resume advice, you'll get 15 different answers. My top advice for writing a resume is keep it concise, focus on accomplishments, and leave room for white space to make it attractive to the eye.

More important is the story you tell, and keeping it fresh:

TAKE THE TV-INTERVIEW APPROACH.
In a TV interview, a person typically gets no more than 20 to 40 seconds to make a point. That's the goal here: capture the most salient information about your recent accomplishments, quickly and concisely.

DO SOME TIMED BRAINSTORMING.
Give yourself a series of timed exercises that help you get to the most important material. Set a timer for two minutes and write five bullet points. These points should include things about yourself, what you have done, a time when you overcame a challenge or exceeded your goals, your five biggest accomplishments, and two biggest failures.

SEARCH AND DESTROY FOR MEANINGLESS PHRASES.
As you review and revise your resume, scan for those meaningless words. Never ever describe yourself as "innovative," "energetic," "a team player," "a self-starter," or "a good communicator." These are so overused that they have become meaningless.

UPDATE YOUR RESUME AND LINKEDIN PROFILE.
Using this script, update your resume and your LinkedIn profile. Proofread carefully by reading aloud. You don't want a typo to knock you out of consideration.

NO SHOTGUNNING ALLOWED.
You may love your shiny new resume, but resist sending it out blindly to everyone and anyone. Trust me, it will be deleted. Your resume is best viewed as a calling card after you've targeted and networked to a warm introduction.

Those who dive into this homework distinguish themselves far more convincingly than the rest. You'd be surprised how many people get this wrong. I have seen resumes of CEOs from large companies that are not much more than one job description listed after another. Nowhere do these documents list the leadership qualities and accomplishments that give perspective to a 20-plus-year career.

Your Stretch Assignment

TEST-DRIVE YOUR RESUME

Ask for feedback from a mentor or trusted advisor. Don't rely on a spouse/partner, friend, or family member—it's hard to get unbiased feedback from them, and criticism can make the relationship awkward. Ask someone who knows you professionally, whose opinion you value, whether your resume reflects who you are and what you bring to an organization.

In an ideal world, you'll never have to pull your resume out of mothballs: you continually review, revise, and refresh this document on an ongoing basis whether or not you're on the market.

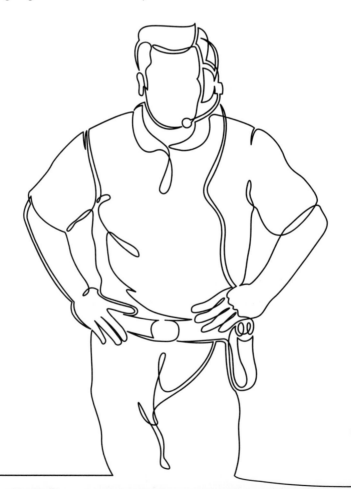

STEP 5

PREP FOR THE INTERVIEW

You aren't auditioning for *Annie*. But when it comes to interview preparation, most candidates put all their focus on scripting and rehearsing what they're going to say. While you should know your lines, learning them is not the first thing you should do. You need to focus first on your ACT: being **authentic**, making a **connection**, and giving others a **taste** of who you are and what it's like to work with you.

IT'S NOT AN INTERROGATION, EITHER

Focusing on your ACT will also help you control your emotions, which are bound to be mixed and intense—it happens to everyone regardless of level. This was clearly happening with a man I saw recently at a Starbucks: his leg pumped up and down as he shuffled anxiously through his notecards. On top of his table I could clearly see his resume.

"Job interview, huh?" I asked as I approached him.

His eyes bulged from caffeine and desperation. "Yeah, and I really need this job."

"Well, you're not doing yourself any favors." I pointed to his triple red eye (coffee with three shots of espresso). "Take some deep breaths and relax. If you go into the interview looking like this, you're going to blow it."

Now I had his attention. "This is not an interrogation," I told him. "Your goal is to have a conversation with your interviewer—pure and simple."

Conquering the interviewing mental game is crucial now that you're finally at this phase of the 90-Day Career Diet. You're ready—so stop psyching yourself out!

Your Homework
THE MENTAL GAME

Perfect your mental game so you can be at your best at the interview. Otherwise, all your targeting, networking, and resume revising are going to go to waste.

THE DENTIST AND DISNEYLAND.
Most people view interviews as a cross between a trip to Disneyland and a visit to the dentist to have a tooth extracted: while you look forward to it, you also dread it. If you let your imagination run wild, you'll amp up your panic until you can't put two coherent sentences together, or you overcompensate by talking nonstop.

THE OLD STANDARDS.
While you never know what you might be asked, you can count on some version of these old standards as the most likely questions:

> → *Tell me about yourself.* Start with something personal—where you were raised, where you went to school, your family, when you moved to your current city, or why you went into the career you've chosen. Invest a minute in making a connection.

→ ***Tell me about your most recent position.*** Be prepared to discuss what you're doing in a way that's relevant to the position you're seeking. Use brief stories to illustrate key points: challenge, action, result, and lessons learned.

→ ***What's your greatest career accomplishment?*** Tell a 30-second story, highlighting key details. Talk about a problem you overcame or an opportunity you realized.

→ ***What are your strengths?*** Identify two or three strengths and discuss each with a specific example.

AVOID THE DEADLY SINS OF INTERVIEWING.

Your preparation should focus on *you* as well: your appearance, your logistics, how you present yourself. The more you prepare, the better you'll avoid committing one of these deadly sins:

→ ***Dressing like* Dancing with the Stars.** Not every job interview requires a suit, but you still should present yourself as well groomed and professional. Know the difference between business professional and business casual, and when in doubt, dress one step up.

→ ***Arriving late.*** You'd think this one is obvious, but it isn't. Do a practice run so you know where you're going. Arrive well in advance—an hour ahead is fine. Sit in a coffee shop or in your car to relax, then walk into the building 10 to 15 minutes before your appointment.

→ ***Being clueless.*** Do your homework and check out the bios and LinkedIn profiles of your interviewers. Read everything you can about the company, its mission, and its values.

→ ***Winging it.*** You don't want to overrehearse, but you do have to prepare. Have sound bites of your three top accomplishments to tell the interviewer.

→ ***Lying, inflating, and exaggerating.*** If you misrepresent yourself in something small, suddenly everything you say is suspect.

→ ***No questions, thank you.*** You must ask questions—for example, about job responsibilities or how the department functions. Being able to insert your questions into the interview will turn an interview into a conversation.

Your Stretch Assignment
THE FIRST
SEVEN SECONDS

During the first seven seconds or so, the interviewer will make crucial determinations about you, including your likability, your trustworthiness, how assertive or passive you seem, and how well you would fit in with others on the team. Based on this initial determination (which is typically unconscious), your interviewer will decide (probably also unconsciously) whether to help you in the interview by rephrasing questions, giving helpful feedback, or assuring you with verbal and nonverbal cues.

Your ACT can help you make the most of those seven seconds. Do some sleuthing on LinkedIn to see if you share a commonality with your interviewer—maybe the same college, or a passion for a sport or pastime (don't fake this or you'll quickly trip yourself up). Scan for something interesting in the person's office that you can talk about. Don't be a snoop, but if you can see it in the open, it's fair game. This small talk will help forge a connection as you relax and allow the interviewer to get to know you.

Interview prep is crucial. You'll never present your best self if you're jittering with every response. So skip the *Annie* audition, forget the interrogation, and enter into the conversation.

STEP 6

THE FACE-TO-FACE

Now it's go time. All of your hard work on the 90-Day Career Diet—knowing yourself, targeting opportunities, networking, revising your resume, and conquering the mental game of interview prep—is about to pay off. Sure, you need to bring your A game: Did your homework? Check. Polished up your appearance? Check. Arrived in plenty of time? Check.

But as much as you prepare, you're going into the unknown.

BE THE PERFECT GUEST

From the moment you arrive for the interview, you're on with everyone you meet, from the parking-lot attendant to the receptionist to the interviewer. You're friendly and smiling, respectful and hyperaware (which may feel like an odd mix between going to a wedding and attending a funeral). You're on high alert for commonalities—a picture, a piece of art on the wall, sports or collegiate mementos—anything that can help you break the ice with "getting to know you" small talk. If you're in sync with the interviewer, the exchange of information will feel much more relaxed, like a conversation rather than an interrogation.

Some things, however, remain completely out of your control. Some hiring managers are very skilled interviewers, some do OK, and some are just downright awful. Some people stand by a standard Q&A script; others throw in oddball questions. Some do most of the talking. No matter who you wind up getting as an interviewer, you can still come out on top if you follow the playbook.

Your Homework
YOUR PLAYBOOK—THE FIVE INTERVIEWER TYPES

Interviewers fall into five categories based on their style and approach. Knowing how to make the most of your interaction with them will go a long way toward success.

The General. This no-nonsense interviewer will probably sit across from you, keeping the desk or conference table between the two of you. The General is more interested in what you would bring to the job than in your personality and will likely ask short questions and expect concise answers. But you should still look around the General's neat and well-organized office for possible connecting points, such as a photograph, a piece of art, or even the view out the window. Be prepared to relate brief anecdotes and examples that effectively translate how your experience meets the company's needs. And don't forget to ask the General questions.

The Talk-Show Host. This personable interviewer will most likely meet you in an office that reveals his or her style and personality with photos, art, and other glimpses into his or her personal life. The Talk-Show Host will probably sit next to you, which means you'll probably let your guard down—which is the whole point! The Talk-Show Host is less concerned with the details of your experience and focuses more on how well you fit the company's culture and environment. The Talk-Show Host will speak of "us" and emphasize commitment to the company. Respond in kind, and emphasize your people skills.

The Scientist. This analytical interviewer wants to know how you intend to contribute and is less interested in what you're doing now or have done. The Scientist appreciates lengthy, detailed answers, and will probably be frustrated by answers that are too short or lacking specifics. It's all about how well you would do in the job, the skills and experiences you would apply to problems, and the kind of results you can deliver.

The Bumbler. This incompetent interviewer will likely ramble, appear disorganized, and perhaps be unclear about the position you're interviewing for. Be the gracious visitor and share more of the hosting duties by volunteering information and directing the questions as best you can. Proactively summarize your skills and accomplishments so the Bumbler learns the necessary information about you and your skill set.

The Clueless. This befuddled interviewer may not even know what position you're interviewing for. Don't be frustrated by this—just go with it. Stay grounded in your ACT: be authentic, make a connection, and give the interviewer a taste of who you are and what it would be like to work with you. With this approach, even an interview with a clueless manager can be a success.

Your Stretch Assignment
BE MEMORABLE

Take the extra step by standing out in ways that people might not expect. Pick up on perceptions (positive, not negative) or assumptions that people may have about you because of your profession or background. A perfect example is military leaders, who are known for being disciplined, loyal, and mission oriented—all great traits valued by organizations. The "value add" would be for a veteran to showcase these expected qualities plus discuss being a creative, out-of-the-box thinker. That would really stand out. Or a Harvard MBA might balance that very impressive credential with a show of genuine humility and a willingness to learn from everyone. Ask yourself: What would make you appear well-rounded and more memorable?

An interview is like going to a party where you don't know anyone. You never know who's going to show up. So be prepared, be aware, and be flexible.

STEP 7

ON TO THE NEXT ONE

Congratulations, you got the job! Now it's time to think about your next one.

This might strike you as odd, since you haven't even finished your first week yet. But the 90-Day Career Diet isn't a "one and done" exercise, like losing 15 pounds before the next college reunion. It's a lifestyle change, such as committing to a better diet and regular exercise.

Even as you distinguish yourself in your brand-new job, you need to continue the Career Diet. Statistically speaking, you probably won't be in your new job for long. Job tenure keeps shrinking—about four years on average and only one to two years for younger workers. That isn't a sign of dissatisfaction; it's the path of the "career nomad," who is looking to make an impact quickly and then move on. And the best time to get a new job is when you already have one.

LEARN ALL
YOU CAN

The most important rewards from your new job—far more than salary, bonus, or title—are the lessons you learn. One of the main reasons to take a new job is to gain skills and expand your experiences.

Consider the 70-20-10 rule: about 70 percent of your learning and development comes from assignments that stretch you and allow you to learn new skills; 20 percent will be from other people, especially your boss; and 10 percent will be from training and courses. So let your curiosity lead you to commit to continuous learning.

Your Homework

NETWORK, NETWORK, NETWORK

Six degrees of separation—the idea that anyone can be connected to any other person through a chain of acquaintances with no more than five intermediaries—isn't just a theory. It's reality! Over my career, I've seen this played out thousands of times. Now, as you start your new job, your networking should kick up a notch, especially internally as you get to know others across the company and explore the next opportunity.

YOUR NEW COMPANY IS A NETWORK.

Companies have formal organizational charts, policies, and procedures. But the reality is that in almost every company, there's an informal way that things get done. I call this "the informal network." Talk to your peers to figure out this network: Who are the influencers who carry the most weight? How can you best work with them? What do they appreciate or dislike? In every interaction, remember your ACT!

HELP OTHERS FOLLOW YOUR PATH.

Your job change will probably spread through your network like a news flash, especially when you update your LinkedIn profile. This will prompt people to wish you well and also to reach out to you for help and advice. Be a sounding board and a helpful hand. Others helped you; now it's time for some karmic reciprocation.

Your Stretch Assignment

BE AN OUTLIER
IN AN UNCERTAIN WORLD

The one thing we can be sure about is that tomorrow won't look like today. In what's being called the Fourth Industrial Revolution, technological forces of progress are putting stress on how and where we work. Some jobs that exist today will go the way of the blacksmith and the retail clerk. You need to be learning and stretching constantly so you become an outlier in terms of performance.

Your new job isn't an end, it's the beginning. As a career nomad, you're constantly on the move and evolving with every step.

✔ *DOUBLE DOWN ON INDISPENSABILITY.* No one has a crystal ball on their desk. You don't know what's going to happen, whether you're going to receive a surprise promotion or the unwelcome news of downsizing in your department. You cannot prevent things beyond your control. But if you become indispensable, especially to your boss, by being the go-to person who gets things done, you'll come out on top.

✔ *FIND YOUR PLACE IN THE TALENT MOSAIC.* Companies everywhere will still need to attract, develop, and align people who represent a mosaic of talents and abilities—diverse by every definition. Inclusive organizations embrace the multiplicity of differences as a competitive edge for understanding and serving global customers. You want to be part of that mosaic.

✔ *RINSE AND REPEAT.* Go back to the first step of the 90-Day Career Diet—knowing yourself—and do it all again: identifying strengths and weaknesses, connecting with your passion and purpose, targeting opportunities, and networking internally and externally. And always, in every interaction—from a job interview to a colleague conversation—put your ACT in action.

ACKNOWLEDGMENTS

Korn Ferry enables people to become more than their potential. We're the ultimate insiders. This book incorporates more than five decades of Korn Ferry intellectual property and the expertise of a global consulting firm that develops 1.2 million people every year.

Without our 8,500 colleagues worldwide, this book would not have been possible. Many people contributed insights, stories, and enthusiasm to this book.

Finally, all the stories in this book are true or true to life. The names and details have been changed to protect the innocent, the guilty, and everyone in between.

This is not "The End."

Even if you applied every single lesson in this book—every practical step and motivating principle—you would still not be done. Nor should you be. And if you think you are, then it's game over: you're not advancing.

At every phase and stage of your career, you are going to face new challenges. Some of them will relate to people. The names and faces will change, but you'll have difficult bosses and annoying coworkers. You will always need to uncover blind spots. You'll need to learn constantly and hone your right-brain skills, particularly as you work and lead others.

This is really "The Beginning."

A 360-DEGREE APPROACH TO ADVANCING YOUR CAREER

At **KORN FERRY,** we have shown eight million executives how to achieve their career goals. Now, drawing on five decades of expertise, we're offering a new solution to help people who wants to realize their potential: Korn Ferry Advance. Korn Ferry Advance offers a 360-degree approach to professional advancement. We leverage decades of expertise in executive search, assessment, learning and leadership development, and salary negotiation to help people pursue rewarding professional opportunities. Our program is customized to you and your goals, while giving you access to the collective knowledge of Korn Ferry's 8,500 experts. Your Korn Ferry Advance membership includes:

ONE-ON-ONE CAREER ADVANCEMENT → Work with the best in the business. Korn Ferry consultants place a candidate in a new role every three minutes and develop thousands of executives and professionals every month. We know exactly what organizations want. You'll work with a personal advisor who provides customized strategies to advance your career.

SELF-IMPROVEMENT → Korn Ferry Advance offers an in-depth look at your traits, skills, and blind spots. In addition, by applying insights from your assessment, we create development beyond your current career trajectory.

For more resources, coaching, and other help in advancing your career, go to **KFAdvance.com**. Use the code **ADVANCE360** at checkout to receive a 25 percent discount on a Premium membership to Korn Ferry Advance, where you can work with the best to achieve your career goals.

To be Continued